Lost Childhoods

Lost Childhoods

Poverty, Trauma, and Violent Crime in the Post-Welfare Era

MICHAELA SOYER

University of California Press

University of California Press, one of the most distinguished university presses in the United States, enriches lives around the world by advancing scholarship in the humanities, social sciences, and natural sciences. Its activities are supported by the UC Press Foundation and by philanthropic contributions from individuals and institutions. For more information, visit www.ucpress.edu.

University of California Press
Oakland, California

Cataloging-in-Publication Data is on file at the Library of Congress.

ISBN 978-0-520-29670-1 (cloth)
ISBN 978-0-520-29671-8 (paper)
ISBN 978-0-520-96908-7 (e-edition)

27 26 25 24 23 22 21 20 19 18
10 9 8 7 6 5 4 3 2 1

Contents

Acknowledgments   vii

INTRODUCTION   1

1. PUNISHMENT AND THE WELFARE STATE   11

2. THE MAKING OF LIFE-COURSE-PERSISTENT OFFENDERS   22

3. THE END OF CHILDHOOD: PARENTAL DRUG ADDICTION
   AND VIOLENCE   37

4. THE WEAKNESS OF STRONG TIES: EXTREME POVERTY
   AND THE FRACTURE OF CLOSE KINSHIP TIES   52

5. MASCULINITY AND VIOLENCE: PHYSICAL AND
   EMOTIONAL ABUSE AT HOME AND IN THE JUVENILE
   JUSTICE SYSTEM   67

6. LOSING CHILDREN   83

   CONCLUSION AND POLICY IMPLICATIONS   97

Appendix I   105

Appendix II   112

Notes   125

References   131

Index   143

For my parents, Ingeborg and Wolfgang Soyer

Acknowledgments

Most of all I am indebted to the young men I interviewed at SCI Pine Grove. They shared intimate and painful memories with me and vividly described their failures and feelings of shame and desperation. As they recalled their lives, they showed a remarkable level of self-reflection and clarity about their past. I hope that this book does justice to the complexity and dignity of their lives. I am equally grateful to the friends and caregivers who agreed to be interviewed. They graciously allowed me into their homes and helped me to expand my perspective on the young men's lives.

Lost Childhoods is my second book, but for the first time I had to work through data completely independently—without the thoughtful guidance of a dissertation committee. I continue to feel uncertain about the final product, but the many friends and colleagues who supported me throughout this research and writing process helped me to see this project through to its conclusion.

The research for this book was accomplished during my tenure as a postdoctoral scholar at the Justice Center for Research at Penn State University. I want to thank Gary Zajac and Doris McKenzie, who offered me a temporary intellectual home after I graduated from the University of Chicago. I am immensely grateful for the material and intellectual support the Justice Center for Research provided.

When I started my postdoctoral position, taking on a new project seemed daunting, but thanks to a grant from the ASA/NSF Fund for the Advancement of the Discipline, it became possible for me to conceptualize and conduct new research just after I had finished my dissertation. Of the many people who helped me during the data collection phase, I specifically would like to thank Shannon Singer, who diligently transcribed the interviews I conducted. My thanks also go to Steven Matthews. The meeting

I had with him, before I began my interviews at SCI Pine Grove, inspired me to make use of maps and address history during the interview process. Over the course of this research, I often relied on the invaluable advice of my friend and fellow postdoctoral scholar Susan McNeely. Melinda Bell and Pamela McCratic have been the best adoptive aunts our daughters could wish for and I feel very lucky to have met them during this important time in my life.

As most researchers can attest to, it is very challenging to start a new research project when beginning a tenure track position. Lynn Chancer not only offered me my dream job, but also convinced the administration to let me defer my start date at Hunter College for another year. I am grateful for her advocacy and continuous support. At Hunter College I am lucky to be surrounded by fantastic colleagues, whose advice has been invaluable throughout my first years there. I want to thank my current department chair, Erica Chito-Childs, for understanding how difficult it is to balance motherhood, teaching, and research.

Of all friends and colleagues, Danielle Raudenbush has had the greatest impact on the intellectual development of this manuscript. She patiently read several versions of it and ensured that I remained committed to connecting my empirical observations with careful theoretical analysis. Without my parents' presence, it would have been impossible to find the time necessary for finishing this book. They selflessly have taken care of our daughters during summer months and given me the space to do my work. My husband, Ed Silver, took over parenting duties while I conducted interviews. I am thankful for his patience and persistence through the emotional ups and downs of my writing process. I also want to thank my daughters, Cordelia and Rebekka, for reminding me what is really important in life.

My final thanks goes to Andrea Leverentz and Jerry Flores, whose extensive feedback improved the manuscript immeasurably.

Introduction

Only when a man can already perform an act of standing straight does he know what it is like to have a right posture and only then can he summon the idea required for proper execution.
—JOHN DEWEY, *Human Nature and Conduct*, [1922] 1988

Isaac's grandmother remembers that her daughter was "handcuffed to the bed" when she picked up her newborn grandson from the hospital. When Isaac was born in March 1994 his mother was incarcerated. Two years later the State of Pennsylvania passed a law allowing the transfer of juveniles as young as fifteen to the adult criminal justice system. "Act 33" ensures that teenagers who committed violent crimes (for example, robbery, aggravated indecent assault, or murder) can automatically be sentenced as if they were adults.

Isaac was "a good kid," his grandmother recalls, quieter than the other four grandchildren she raised in a mid-sized town in eastern Pennsylvania. Now in her sixties she may never see her grandson again outside of prison walls. Isaac is serving a sentence of twenty to forty years for two counts of manslaughter. Since 2012 he is one of approximately three hundred inmates in a unit specifically designed for youths who are "doing adult time" for crimes they committed when they were younger than eighteen.

Isaac and the twenty-nine other youths I interviewed for this book had grown up long before they arrived at SCI Pine Grove, the remote prison in central Pennsylvania where I met them. Many saw their mothers or fathers succumbing to drugs or alcohol. They witnessed police raiding their homes and watched their fathers, uncles, and older brothers being whisked away to prison. As young children they faced eviction, gun violence, and hunger. They were born during the early to mid-1990s, a decade that saw an unprecedented expansion of the criminal justice system coupled with the disappearance of a robust welfare state.

Criminological theories offer many possible explanations for criminal behavior. Most, at least implicitly, acknowledge the role of rising inequality and concentrated disadvantage. Anomie theory argues that criminal behavior arises because conventional pathways to economic success are blocked

(Merton 1938). Labeling theorists, in contrast, see deviance as a social construct serving those who are already in power (Erikson 1996). Recent work suggests disadvantaged areas offer more opportunities for criminal behavior. Poor neighborhoods lack resources, such as opportunities for legal employment and access to high-quality schools (Massey and Denton 1993; Wilson 2009; Graif, Gladfelter, and Matthews 2014). Growing up poor may also create a level of stress that leads to crime as a coping mechanism (Agnew 1992). Finally, developmental psychologists argue that cognitive deficits related to criminal behavior are more prevalent and less likely to be counteracted in socioeconomically disadvantaged situations than in middle-class families (Moffitt 1993).

Even though research affirms the connection between socioeconomic disadvantage and crime, the individual processes that connect living in poverty and criminal behavior are rarely accounted for in detailed and systematic ways. Criminologists tend to focus on the social processes that mediate the connection between poverty and criminal behavior; for example, peer networks or the absence of collective efficacy on the neighborhood level (Sharkey, Besbris, and Friedson 2016). Sociologists shy away from explicitly addressing self-destructive behaviors of the poor, fearing it may be constructed as victim-blaming (Bourgois 2002).

Proponents of control theory could argue that the young men in this book lack "self-control" in every aspect of their lives (Gottfredson and Hirschi 1990). It is also possible to identify a "culture of poverty" that has been transmitted within families across multiple generations (Lewis 1975).

In *Lost Childhoods* I set aside the ambivalent concept of "culture" and the equally malleable term "self-control." Instead I approach the data from a structural perspective. By embedding the narratives in the structural and institutional changes that swept through the United States during the 1990s, the cases I present become a symbol for three decades of misguided welfare and criminal justice policies.

In the following pages I show how extreme deprivation shapes criminal trajectories. In the absence of a robust welfare state, the juvenile and criminal justice systems are the only centralized state bureaucracies offering social services. Zimring (2005) and others (e.g., Hayne 2010) have long argued that criminal justice institutions are ill-equipped to fulfill the dual function of punishment and welfare. It is almost impossible to provide consistent social support to marginalized populations from within a punitive organizational framework (Sufrin 2017; Soyer 2016; Comfort 2008; Platt 1977, Stuart 2016).

The young men's extreme deprivation was rarely visible to anyone outside of their families. They had learned to mistrust government agencies.[1]

During the mid-1980s President Ronald Reagan infamously claimed that "I'm from the government and I'm here to help" were the nine most terrifying words in the English language.[2] More than thirty years later this statement rings true not to the farmers Reagan addressed, but to those families who need government support the most.[3] The young men recall that having someone "from the government" at your doorstep usually means bad news: Children are taken out of their homes and placed into foster care; apartments are raided and family members arrested (Goffman 2014). The absence of a welfare state, in combination with a ballooning criminal justice system, alienates disadvantaged families and makes it even more difficult for them to move out of poverty.

More than any other legislation, the Social Security Act of 1935 affirmed the collective responsibility of the United States for its most vulnerable members—the elderly and children.[4] The Great Depression accelerated the establishment of a comprehensive welfare bureaucracy, but even before the economic meltdown in 1929, public discourse had shifted toward an expansion of the social safety net (Garland 2001). Already in 1922 John Dewey published his foundational work, *Human Nature and Conduct*, where he argued that the individual and society are inseparably intertwined. According to Dewey individual shortcomings originate in malformed habits that develop in relation to a dysfunctional social environment. Today, Dewey's "Of Human Conduct" offers a philosophical alternative to the current hyperindividualistic and increasingly chauvinistic political discourse.

The data I present in this book calls for revisiting some of the ideas that emerged in the early twentieth century and became institutionalized during the decades of postwar prosperity (Garland 2001). Even though the contemporary United States could not be ideologically further removed from Franklin D. Roosevelt's "Great Society," finding ways of increasing access to social services beyond the criminal justice system is necessary for fiscal and humanitarian reasons (Sufrin 2017).

Aspiring to make the case for expanding nonpunitive welfare provisions, *Lost Childhoods* develops two different lines of argumentation. The first part of the book focuses on the brutalizing force that unmitigated poverty has had on the young men I interviewed. The final chapters emphasize the flawed ways in which the juvenile and criminal justice systems address the respondents' social welfare needs.

The staggering extent of traumatic events the young men experienced during their childhoods is the common denominator of the data I collected. Most families I visited were entangled in a web of hardship and tragedy that often accompanies the very poor (Desmond 2016). The young men therefore suffered from a double disadvantage: Their traumatic experiences were closely related to their families' abject poverty. At the same time their parents' severe disadvantage made it highly unlikely that any of the trauma the young men lived through was therapeutically addressed in its aftermath. The life-course narratives show how aggregated trauma and hardship have shaped the respondents' criminal trajectories. The interventions of the juvenile justice system often happened too late, and even if the system provided important social services, juvenile justice institutions still victimized the young men.

LIMITATIONS

Before diving into the details of the theoretical arguments and empirical analysis, it is necessary to briefly address the limitations of this project.[5] There are so many contingent, interconnected variables that shaped the young men's choices that it is impossible to draw definitive conclusions about what would have happened if the teenagers had grown up in a society that prioritizes social support for its poorest citizens. Because of these uncertainties, I cannot satisfyingly answer the "chicken and egg" question of what ultimately caused the young men's violent offending (LeBel et al. 2008). I can, however, draw comparisons between the different cases and point out the important similarities that emerge over the course of the analysis.

The lack of a counterfactual group—for example, young men who grew up poor but did not commit crimes—is another conceptual weakness. Being born into extreme poverty does not inevitably lead to a life of crime. Research has shown that children have different levels of resilience depending on, for example, cognitive abilities, self-esteem, and parenting competence (Vanderbilt-Adriance and Shaw 2008; Masten 2001; Masten and Coatsworth 1998). The young men I interviewed are undoubtedly extreme cases. I treat the thirty original respondents as a Weberian ideal type. It is their outlier status that allows me to focus on how criminal behavior and extreme poverty interrelate (Weber 1949).

RESEARCH SETTING

The main protagonists of *Lost Childhoods* are thirty young men adjudicated as adults for crimes they committed while they were still underage. All of them were held at the State Correctional Institution (SCI) Pine Grove in a unit specifically designed for what the state terms Young Adult Offenders (YAO). I was able to interview them over the course of three months beginning in April 2014. I met with twenty-nine participants three times during this time frame. One respondent was sent to the restricted housing unit and could only complete one interview. The interviews focused on different aspects of their life-course, from early childhood until their current life situation. At the end of our final interview I asked the respondents for the phone numbers and addresses of family members and friends potentially willing to be interviewed. I was not allowed to compensate the young men for their time. Outside respondents received a thirty-dollar gift card for their participation.

Geographically, the young men's families and friends clustered around the urban areas of Pennsylvania: Harrisburg, Pittsburgh, and Philadelphia. I was able to interview thirty-one family members and friends. I could not track down family or friends for seven of the original respondents. The missing data is related to geographical location, unavailability of current contact information, and in one case to language barriers. When phone numbers provided by the young men proved to be disconnected, I usually stopped by families' homes for recruitment visits. Many of these visits directly led to an interview. For families that lived more than four hours' driving distance from where I was located, this strategy became logistically and economically infeasible. Some families did not keep in touch with their sons. In these cases the original respondents did not have current phone numbers or addresses for potential interview partners on the outside. I also refrained from recruiting one relative because her grandson indicated that she only speaks Spanish. In total I conducted 120 interviews for this study.

In addition to narrative data, I had access to so-called "integrated case summary files" assembled by the Pennsylvania Department of Corrections (PADOC). These files contain the inmates' social, educational, and work histories, as well as several risk measures collected by PADOC. They also cover both narratives of the juveniles recalling their crime and official police reports.[6] Table 1 summarizes the respondents' basic demographic information. It includes the offense that led to their incarceration at SCI Pine Grove and the sentence they received, as well as the approximate time they had already served at the prison when I first interviewed them.

OVERVIEW OF THE BOOK

Lost Childhoods contextualizes the personal narratives of the so-called "Young Adult Offenders" within the larger structural developments that defined U.S. society over the past three decades. Chapters 1 and 2 provide the historical and theoretical framework for this study. The empirical

TABLE 1: Research Participants

Name	Race	Year of Birth	Conviction	Min–Max Sentence*	Time at SCI Pine Grove*	Friend/ Relative Interviewed
Alexander	Latino	1993	Theft	2–4 years	2 years	1
Andrew	Mixed	1993	Burglary	2–6 years	2 years	2
Austin	Black	1994	Arson	1–5 years	6 months	1
Blake	Black	1992	Drug Manufacture/Sale/Delivery	1–5 years	3½ years	1
Bryan	Black	1993	Carrying Firearm w/o License	2–5 years	2 years	None
Connor	Mixed	1994	Robbery	3–10 years	2 years	None
Dylan	Black	1993	Murder 3rd Degree	25–50 years	2 years	1
Elijah	Black	1992	Drug Manufacture/Sale/Delivery	3–7 years	3 years	1
Gabriel	Black	1993	Robbery	4–8 years	2 years	1
Henry	White	1994	Theft	2–4 years	1 year	1
Isaac	Black	1994	Murder 3rd Degree	20–40 years	1 year	1
Jaxon	Black	1994	Robbery	2–8 years	3 years	1
Jeremiah	Black	1993	Aggravated Assault	4–8 years	4 years	2
Jesus	Latino	1994	Aggravated Harassment	2–4 years	1 year	None
John	Mixed	1994	Robbery	2–3 years	1½ years	1
Jordan	Black	1993	Robbery	4–8 years	3 years	1
Joshua	Black	1993	Robbery	2–5 years	2 years	1
Josiah	Black	1993	Burglary	3–6 years	1 year	1

Name	Race	Year	Crime	Sentence Range	Time Served	Number*
Julian	White	1992	Aggravated Assault	4–17 years	3 years	2
Kayden	Black	1994	Aggravated Assault	2–4 years	1 year	2
Luke	White	1994	Robbery	3–10 years	1½ years	1
Marc	Black	1994	Aggravated Assault	9–20 years	4 years	2
Mateo	Latino	1993	Aggravated Assault	2–5 years	2 years	2
Miguel	Latino	1992	Robbery	5–10 years	3 years	None
Nate	Asian	1993	Robbery of Motor Vehicles	4–8 years	2 years	None
Oliver	White	1994	Receiving Stolen Property	9 months–3 years	1 year	1
Robert	White	1993	Sale or Transfer of Firearms	15–30 years	3 years	2
Samuel	Black	1994	Robbery	2–4 years	1 year	None
Tyler	Black	1992	Robbery	5–12 years	3 years	None
William	White	1994	Aggravated Assault	4–8 years	1 year	2

NOTE: Names are altered to protect the identity of the research participants.
* Numbers are rounded up.

chapters 3 and 4 cover the different traumatic events that in the aggregate hastened the young men's descent into criminal behavior. Chapters 5 and 6 emphasize the ambivalent role the criminal justice system plays in the lives of extremely disadvantaged families. These final two chapters focus on how the teenagers' incarceration has simultaneously provided a form of relief while also traumatizing the young men and their families further.

Chapter 1, "Punishment and the Welfare State," reviews the parallel dismantling of the welfare state and the expansion of the criminal and juvenile justice systems during the mid-1990s. I briefly summarize how welfare reform has impacted the poorest strata of America society and provide a detailed accounting of the nationwide criminalization of teenagers. I describe the pains of incarceration the young men experienced at SCI Pine Grove and conclude the chapter by pointing to the long-term social implications of ending welfare and expanding the criminal justice system.

Chapter 2, "The Making of Life-Course-Persistent Offenders," summarizes prior work on the effects of childhood trauma on the life-course of children. I focus in particular on the relationship between childhood trauma and later criminal behavior. This chapter provides a general overview of the different types of traumatic experience that have shaped the life-course of the young men. I maintain that the respondents often faced a combination of what Terr (1991) calls Type I (a singular event) and Type II (prolonged suffering) trauma that can significantly alter someone's perception of risk, decision-making abilities, and the capacity to regulate emotions. This chapter shows that childhood trauma was able to inflict its full impact on the young men's life-course because most families did not have access to mental health services that could have intervened proactively.

The young men I interviewed came of age years after crack consumption peaked in American inner cities. Their lives were nevertheless significantly impacted by their parents' drug consumption. Chapter 3, "The End of Childhood: Parental Drug Addiction and Violence," focuses on four African American men whose criminal behavior was closely connected to their parents' drug addiction. I show that these four young men suffered from a reverse "maturity gap." Adolescence-limited offenders, Moffitt (1993) argues, become involved in criminal behavior because they want to close the gap between inhabiting an adult body and still being considered a child socially. The young men I portray in this chapter experienced the exact opposite. They were forced to make independent decisions when they were still children. At that time they were neither physically nor cognitively ready to take care of themselves, or to foresee the consequences of their behavioral choices. Experiencing an unusual autonomy at a young age made it even more difficult for the respondents to be receptive to juvenile justice interventions. The young men in this chapter may never have consumed crack, but the destructive force of the drug shaped their life-course nonetheless.

Chapter 4, "The Weakness of Strong Ties: Extreme Poverty and the Fracture of Close Kinship Ties," focuses on the destabilizing effect poverty has on strong familial ties between children and caregivers. While middle-class children remain financially connected to their parents at least until they finish college in their mid-twenties, the families I met tend to sever emotional and financial ties to children during the early years of adolescence. The young men I interviewed experienced repeatedly that the ties to adults in their lives are fragile. Being able to stay in the parental home could not be taken for granted, nor could financial or emotional support. Aside from the traumatic impact of losing a caregiver, lacking parental supervision generates opportunities for crime and encourages the respondents to engage in criminal behavior to fulfill their basic needs (Felson and Cohen 1979; Agnew 1992).

Chapter 5, "Masculinity and Violence: Physical and Emotional Abuse at Home and in the Juvenile Justice System," shows how the juvenile justice system perpetuates traumatic experiences the respondents lived through in their homes. I describe how a kind of "outsider masculinity" (Reich 2010) fulfilled multiple functions by allowing the young men to rationalize the violence they committed as well as the abuse and neglect they experienced at the hands of others. I reveal that the Glen Mills Schools, an institution conceived to reform and support struggling teenagers, continued to feed into an outdated concept of masculinity that fosters abuse and violence. This chapter focuses on the young men's unacknowledged abuse that took place before they were transferred to the adult criminal justice system, and serves as an important reminder that even as the juvenile justice system provides urgently needed social services, it further victimizes children.

Chapter 6, "Losing Children," switches perspectives from the young men to their immediate social circle. I show how incarceration of their sons, nephews, or grandsons impacts families. I specifically focus on the ambivalence some parents feel toward the criminal and juvenile justice systems. Mothers may recognize that the systems offer immediate support but also that incarceration continues to leave their sons ill-equipped to lead productive lives.

I portray mothers' disappointment in their sons, as well as their regret and shame over what they perceive as having failed as a parent. I also juxtapose different coping mechanisms, from disconnection and disappointment to regular visits and daily contact with inmates. Finally, I argue that financial resources are strongly related to the ability of families to maintain a connection to the incarcerated young men. Being too poor to pay for a bus ticket or to accept a collect call from prison thus is often the final blow to already fragile ties (Comfort 2008). Expending resources on someone who is facing decades in prison is a luxury for families who have to worry about having enough money to pay rent or to put food on the table.

The young men I introduce in this book grew up in families who have been trapped in poverty for generations. Almost twenty years ago Duncan et al. (1998: 421) argued that "the elimination of deep and persistent poverty during a child's early years" is crucial for raising achievement levels of children coming from disadvantaged families. When the young men were born, a centralized social support system for struggling families had been almost completely eliminated. The respondents' early childhoods were shaped by the fallout of welfare reform—a bill Senator Edward Kennedy famously referred to as "legislative child abuse." When welfare "as we know it" ended, poverty unleashed its full force on already extremely disadvantaged families (Edin and Shaefer 2015).

As young children the Pine Grove inmates had already confronted housing and food insecurity, parental drug addiction, domestic violence, and untreated mental illness. Over the course of this book I shed light on the different ways childhood trauma and abject poverty connect to the chronic criminal behavior that landed the respondents in the Young Adult Offender program.

I maintain that sentencing reform and addressing the racial bias of the U.S. criminal justice system are insufficient to improve the lives of justice-involved youths. The social problems of mass incarceration and criminalization of disadvantaged youths will not be solved unless we take seriously the damage that severe economic pressure inflicts on poor families. Like the young men I interviewed, many prisoners have not only lost significant years behind prison walls, but will continue to hover at the very bottom of the socioeconomic strata after their release (Pager 2003; Loopo and Western 2005; Massoglia 2008; Western et al 2015). Rebuilding a strong welfare state is therefore indispensable for those who reenter society without any meaningful social, economic, or cultural capital (Bourdieu 2001).

1. Punishment and the Welfare State

Welfare and punishment have been intimately connected from the moment prisons and poor houses took shape over 150 years ago (Rothman 1971). The distribution of welfare has always been an occasion to discipline those deviating from whatever the majority has deemed acceptable behavior (Platt 1977; Fox-Piven and Cloward 1993).[1] In the twenty-first century the entanglement of welfare provision and punishment remains relevant for two reasons.

Firstly, the population served by both institutions continues to overlap significantly. Those who are punished for criminal behavior often struggle with socioeconomic disadvantage. Children who grow up poor are more likely to be exposed to multiple adverse factors, peer influences, unstable homes, and substandard schooling that in aggregate increase their susceptibility to criminal behavior (Fergusson, Swain-Campbell, and Horwood 2004). The poor also tend to live in highly policed neighborhoods (Harcourt 2013). Although evidence is mixed, some research has shown that low SES (socioeconomic status) individuals face harsher sentences than wealthier defendants (Chambliss 1969; Thornberry 1973; Chiricos and Waldo 1975; Stolzenberg and D'Alessio 1994).

Secondly, the provision of centralized social services by the government outside of criminal justice institutions has ceased to exist. The criminal justice system is the only state bureaucracy present in the lives of those who suffer extreme poverty. It has fallen to prisons and jails to tend to their inmates' physical and mental health, as well as their educational needs that have been neglected on the outside (Sufrin 2017; Stuart 2016).

As a result, the growth of the criminal justice system and the decline of the welfare state cannot be understood independently from one another. The 1970s marked the decline of the Keynesian economy and the beginnings of the punitive turn in the United States and the United Kingdom. As memories of large-scale unemployment receded into the background and the working class experienced unprecedented prosperity, welfare bureaucracy seemed to create rather than solve problems. Welfare, its critics argued, disincentivized entering the labor force and encouraged government dependency (Garland 2001).

In the United States the decades-long process of undermining the welfare state pivoted in 1996 when President Clinton, with the stroke of a pen, ended one of the most significant legislative components of the New Deal, Aid for Families with Dependent Children (AFDC). As welfare was dismantled, fighting crime became an issue of national importance. The federal "Three Strikes Law," enacted in 1994, would drive incarceration rates to unprecedented levels (Western 2006). Roughly a year later Dilulio (1995) coined the term "super-predators." In his now infamous essay he wrote about young offenders with "vacant stares" and "remorseless eyes" who were too frightening to study. Today, mass incarceration and the decline of the welfare state have left the criminal justice system as the only government institution legitimately able to provide educational and health services to those who have fallen through the cracks.

The organizational restructuring of both systems defined the life-course of the thirty original respondents. They were born after welfare had ended but are still old enough to experience the full force of the punitive turn. What we rather abstractly describe as "mass incarceration" and "welfare reform" brackets the individual narratives of the young men I met at SCI Pine Grove. It is this specific contraction of welfare, the simultaneous expansion of incarceration, and eventual incorporation of welfare provision into criminal justice institutions that have shaped the young men's pathways into crime.

"THE END OF WELFARE AS WE KNOW IT"

Dismantling welfare received strong support across party lines. Voices of dissent were reserved for old-timers such as long-serving senators Edward Kennedy and Patrick Moynihan. The Personal Responsibility and Work Opportunity Reconciliation Act (PRWORA) cleared the House and the Senate without a challenge (Toner 1995). In August 1996, Aid to Families with Dependent Children (AFDC) was official replaced by Temporary Assistance to Needy Families (TANF). "Temporary" may well be the most important aspect of the AFDC replacement. The federal government mandated that states are not allowed to use TANF block grants to aid families for longer than 60 months. Limiting lifetime eligibility for government support to five years obliterated welfare as a permanent safety net and converted it into a temporary "back-to-work" program (Edin and Shaefer 2015; Wacquant 2008b; Moffitt 2008).

Twenty years later, the results of cutting back support for the poorest American citizens are mixed. Caseloads have been significantly reduced. Single mothers have seen an increase in workforce participation and a rise in household income. Programs like the Earned Income Tax Credit (EIC) have also provided important work incentives. Dependency on traditional welfare programs has been reduced to such an extent that TANF expenditure ranks behind the costs for EIC, food stamps, and subsidized housing (Moffitt 2008).

While the numbers appear to prove scenarios of large-scale deprivation wrong, there is a wrinkle in these seemingly positive developments. Life for the poorest bracket of single mothers, for example, has become harder post–welfare reform. The new programs encouraged those who could work to enter the workforce but left few options for people who, for one reason or another, cannot remain employed over the long term. Finally, welfare reform left almost no provision for the childless, unmarried, and unskilled segment of the population (Moffitt 2008).

In their recent work Edin and Shaefer have taken a closer look at this forgotten population. In *$2 A Day: Living on Almost Nothing in America* they describe the life of those "1.5 millions households with 3 million children" who have to make do on two dollars per day per person (Edin and Shaefer 2015). Describing the lives of eighteen families in depth, they show that desperation and disaster are these families' constant companions. Residential instability, job insecurity, and little to no access to government support programs created a "web of exploration" that was impossible to escape (ibid.).

The sociodemographic background of the families Edin and Shaefer followed is very similar to the families of the young men I interviewed. Most of the respondents grew up in households headed by single mothers. The African American and Latino youths grew up in segregated, resource-poor neighborhoods (Massey and Denton 1993). The white youths lived in families that were left behind by mechanization and globalization. Growing up in a post-welfare society meant the young men had the odds stacked against them from early childhood on. The political priorities of the late 1990s, a time of economic growth and prosperity, left childhood poverty largely unaddressed. Instead government funds were allocated to ever-expanding criminal and juvenile justice systems.

PENAL WELFARISM AND MASS INCARCERATION

Social scientists have written extensively about this dual institutional upheaval during the mid-1990s. David Garland argues that the era of rehabilitation-centered criminal justice policies came to an end during the mid-1970s. "Penal welfarism" was replaced with a highly punitive system of mass incarceration. Garland (2001) observes that the utility of rehabilitative approaches to crime that had dominated the previous decades came under intense scrutiny by the mid-1970s. Martinson's famous article "What Works? Questions and Answers about Prison Reform," offered a scathing view of rehabilitative programs. "With few and isolated exceptions," he wrote, "the rehabilitative efforts that have been reported so far have had no appreciable effect on recidivism" (1974: 25). Following Martinson's assessment, the U.S. and U.K. criminal justice systems began to abandon the rehabilitative ideal and instead focused on segregation and control of those deemed incorrigible and too dangerous to be a part of modern society (Garland 2001: 102).

In *Punishing the Poor* Wacquant observes that the U.S. government has lumped welfare recipients and criminals together as the "undesirable poor." He maintains, "welfare revamped as workfare and prison stripped of its rehabilitative pretension now form a single organizational mesh" (2009: 288). The growing carceral state in combination with a deconstructed welfare regime subdues those who have been rendered obsolete in the neoliberal economy. With the marginalized population under control, globalized and deregulated capitalism has free rein and continues to expand its reach (ibid., 304f).

Like Wacquant, Soss, Fording, and Schram (2011) perceive neoliberalism and paternalism as the defining aspects of contemporary poverty governance. They suggest that neoliberals have not abolished but rather hijacked political and civic institutions. While operational strategies may have been altered, these political and social entities retain their authority and neoliberalism has developed into a disciplinary regime in its own right.

In contrast to Wacquant, Soss et al. affirm historical continuity between the different forms of welfare governance. Contemporary restrictions and stigma related to receiving welfare, they argue, resonate with traditional strategies of managing the poor. While welfare may take the form of tax incentives like the Earned Income Tax Credit, generating economic pressure to force people into low-paying jobs is a historically tested form of social and behavioral control.

More recent scholarship addressing the entanglement of welfare and punishment tries to find alternatives to the mass incarceration paradigm. In her ethnography about women's health care in a California jail, Carolyn Sufrin (2017) notes the careful balance that nurses and doctors strike as they manage the health problems of vulnerable populations. As Sufrin summarizes poignantly: "[Jail] . . . routinely provides them [inmates] respite from the danger of the streets, in ways public assistance, free clinics, and nonprofit social service agencies have failed to" (47). In *A Dream Denied* I also observe that the juvenile justice systems in Boston and Chicago are the only government institutions providing desperately needed support for disadvantaged families (Soyer 2016). As Phelps (2011) points out, the U.S. criminal justice system never completely ceased providing rehabilitative services. Criminal justice institutions maintained at least a limited commitment to rehabilitation of offenders even as the official rhetoric overwhelmingly adhered to a "lock-them-up-and-throw-away-the-key" approach.[2]

During those decades that have seen a dramatic increase in incarceration rates, the U.S. Supreme Court also continued to affirm prisoners' right to health care under the Eighth Amendment.[3] As a result, prisons and jails are able to offer health services that are not universally accessible on the outside. The Young Adult Offender Program at SCI Pine Grove is no exception. It at once symbolizes the misguided moral panic about "super-predators" and the attempt to address the young men's educational deficits and therapeutic needs.

Dylan, for example, realized for the first time that he could be suffering from PTSD (post-traumatic stress disorder) when he talked to a counselor on his unit. Others are able to work toward their GED and may even be able to learn a trade. The inmates can enroll in carpentry or custodial maintenance programs. The program, however, remains punitive at its core. The pains of incarceration were especially acute for those who had to serve long sentences. Robert was sentenced to fifteen to thirty years for transferring illegal firearms when he was seventeen. He knows that life will be very different by the time he will be eligible for parole. He is afraid that he won't be able to find his place in society after he has spent his formative years in prison. Robert also wonders whether or not he will be able to handle being free again. He does not know if he is able to exercise self-control without the constant supervision of a carceral institution. Most devastating for him, however, is that he will have nobody to return to: "Once my grandma dies," he says, "I don't really got much."

Isaac, on the other hand, does want to dwell on the long-term implications of his sentence. When I interviewed him, he had only served one year of his twenty-to-thirty-year sentence for third-degree murder. "I ain't trying to sit here and think about it and keep thinking about it and drive myself crazy about it," he says. Dylan, who is serving a sentence of twenty-five to fifty years, is more solemn. Even though he has only been in Pine Grove for two years, he has already lost touch with almost everybody on the outside. "I got a lot of time," he says, and adds: "When I was out there, I was doing stuff for everybody, but like everybody forget what you did." He is trying to appeal his case. "I'm trying to get some time back . . . 'Cause I got twenty-five. I got twenty-five to fifty. Twenty-five to fifty years. That's so fucking long." Dylan will be forty-two by the time he becomes parole eligible. The inmates who are serving long-term sentences, like Robert, profit far less from the rehabilitative programs SCI Pine Grove offers to its underage inmates. Knowing that he still has to spend at least a decade in prison makes it difficult for Robert to take programs seriously that are supposed to prepare him for reentry.

The young men I interviewed symbolize the paradox of a criminal justice system that almost inevitably continues to fulfill caretaking functions. As an institution SCI Pine Grove recognizes the vulnerability of teenage offenders and thus segregates them from the adult population. Nevertheless, the prison still has to enforce punishment according to the rules of the adult criminal justice system.

CRIMINALIZING YOUTHS

For the majority of recorded human history children and adults were considered to be functionally equivalent. Even when Romantic writers portrayed childhood as a sacred state of freedom and innocence, child labor was an essential part of modernizing Western societies (Cunningham and Viazzo 1996). Just as children were working alongside adults, they were also punished according to adult standards. It was only in 1899 that the "child saving movement" gained sufficient traction to successfully lobby for the foundation of the first juvenile court in Chicago, Illinois (Platt 1977).

Early proponents of a separate juvenile justice system envisioned a court that would "uplift" young people by addressing their social problems rather than ostracizing or criminalizing them (Mack 1909; Mead 1918). This balance between punishment and welfare provision has always been difficult to maintain for the courts (Zimring 2005). The 1967 U.S. Supreme Court decision resolved the tension between rehabilitation and punishment in favor of the latter. *In re Gault* established "due process standards" for the juvenile court and required that lawyers be present during court proceedings. While the decision afforded necessary protections for underage offenders, it also encouraged further criminalization of teenagers. As the twentieth century drew to a close, so-called transfer laws further undermined the premise of a separate juvenile justice system. These amendments opened a loophole for circumventing the age of criminal responsibility and trying more juveniles in adult court.[4]

Most states have multiple avenues for transferring underage teenagers to the adult criminal justice system. Generally these mechanisms can be subsumed into three categories: judicial waivers, prosecutorial discretion, and statutory exclusion. Judicial waivers allow juvenile court judges to transfer cases on an individual basis to the criminal court. Prosecutorial discretion, on the other hand, puts the juvenile's fate into the hand of the prosecutor. Certain offenses can be tried either in adult or juvenile court, and the prosecutor decides where to file charges. The third mechanism, statutory exclusion, in contrast, minimizes judicial discretion. The law defines a set of offenses that have to be heard in criminal court, even if the offender is underage. Additionally all states have certain age limits after which teenagers assume criminal responsibility and juvenile court ceases to be an option even for misdemeanors (Griffin et al. 2011).

The age of criminal responsibility poses a challenge in itself as it varies significantly from state to state. Until very recently, for example, New York was one of two states in which any offender sixteen or older had to be tried in adult court. On April 10, 2017, after a lengthy "raise the age campaign" fueled by the high-profile suicide of Kalif Browder, a former juvenile inmate at Riker's Island, Governor Andrew Cuomo established eighteen as the new age of criminal responsibility across the state. Certain transfer laws, nevertheless, remain in place. Children thirteen or older who are charged with a felony begin their proceedings in criminal court. They are transferred back to family court after thirty days. However, under "extraordinary circumstances," for example regarding a violent felony, the district attorney may leave the case under the jurisdiction of the adult court system.[5]

Aron Kupchik (2006) diagnoses the dilemma faced by states like New York when they blend juvenile and criminal justice systems. These hybrid solutions, Kupchik argues, are a response to the inherent contradiction of sending teenagers, who are not fully accountable for their actions, to the adult court system. Trying to negotiate this tension, many criminal justice systems resort to measurements that mimic the juvenile system yet are administered far less efficiently (12–20).

The juvenile and criminal justice systems in Pennsylvania also maintain a hybrid setup similar to the recent legislative changes in New York. In 1995 Pennsylvania introduced Act 33 into the judicial code. This amendment allows for an automatic transfer of juveniles fifteen or older who have committed certain felonies.[6] Additionally, teenagers who have committed a felony may be transferred to the adult criminal justice system if the judge finds that sending the defendant to criminal court is in the public interest. This may be the case for repeat offenders who have failed to respond to juvenile justice interventions.[7]

Act 33 was a direct response to the public discourse initiated by Dilulio's (1995) predictions about the rising numbers of teenagers "perfectly capable of committing the most heinous acts of physical violence for the most trivial reasons."[8] Like many state governments, Pennsylvania wanted to be prepared for this impending wave of extremely violent offenders and began the construction of a prison designed solely for housing this population. The price tag for this maximum-security prison, SCI Pine Grove, in the eastern part of the state was $71 million. By the time the prison was set to open, it was already painfully obvious that the predicted wave of juvenile violence never materialized. Two-thirds of the five-hundred-bed facility remained empty.[9]

Today the prison has designated youthful offender units filled with approximately three hundred youths, about thirty of whom are under the age of eighteen. Every male juvenile sentenced under Act 33 is sent to SCI Pine Grove. (The handful of women sentenced as adults are held at the women's prison SCI Muncy.) Once an inmate has turned twenty-two he ages out of the program and is transferred into the adult population. Ideally he will be relocated closer to where his family lives. Some inmates spend their full sentence length in the youth tract while others remain there only for the first few years of their prison stay.

Even before the groundbreaking of SCI Pine Grove in 1998, a large body of research had already discredited the practice of adjudicating juveniles in adult court. In 1996 Jeffrey Fagan matched juvenile offenders tried in juvenile courts in New Jersey with youths in New York who were tried in criminal court for equivalent offenses. He found that the recidivism rate of the New Jersey teenagers was significantly lower than that of the teenagers who were tried as adults in New York. His results resonate with Bishop et al.'s (1996) analysis of crime data from Florida, who found that being transferred to the adult system increased recidivism rates. Jensen and Metsger (1994) question the deterrent effect of automatic transfer laws, like the one utilized in Pennsylvania. Their time series analysis of crime data in Idaho, before and after the automatic transfer of juveniles was instituted, shows no effect on the number of violent crimes committed by juveniles.

Recent work provides more nuanced perspective but still calls into question the overall usefulness of trying juveniles in criminal courts. In their meta-analysis of research on juvenile transfer laws, Zane et al. (2016a) argue that the dearth of studies makes it extremely challenging to assess the impact that being transferred to adult court has on recidivism. Yet, they argue that the complex juvenile transfer laws are unlikely to have any deterrent effect. Teenagers often do not understand the circumstances of their sentence. Neither can they anticipate the conditions of confinement in an adult facility.

In another meta-analysis, Zane et al. (2016b) show that race plays an increasingly complicated role in who gets transferred from juvenile to an adult court setting. Overall, race seems to be unrelated to waiver decisions. However, the heterogeneity of the results indicates that race may impact waiver decisions in obscure ways. The race effect in the studies they analyzed, for example, varied depending on the analytical strategy and the recency of the results.

ECONOMIC COSTS OF SENDING CHILDREN TO STATE PRISON

In addition to the questionable utility of incarcerating juveniles as adults, the costs of managing a juvenile population in the adult system are prohibitively high. They are likely to rise even further as facilities adapt to the standards set by the Prison Rape Elimination Act (PREA). PREA mandates specific training standards, puts limitations on cross-gender searches, and requires the accessibility of mental health services in case a juvenile inmate reports sexual abuse (Lahey 2016).[10]

The Pennsylvania Department of Corrections spent $33,000 annually per inmate during the fiscal year 2009–10.[11] I was unable to obtain detailed numbers about the program costs for the YAO program per inmate. Looking at other similar programs is an indication that costs balloon once juveniles are held in adult facilities. Michele Deitch et al. (2009) report that Rhode Island spent $100,000 for every juvenile housed in an adult facility.

To reach a valid conclusion concerning the costs of holding juveniles in the adult system versus keeping them in juvenile justice facilities, we would need to estimate the indirect costs of incarcerating underage offenders in adult prisons. This means costs and savings that accrue through higher or lower recidivism rates and the impact a criminal record has on future earning potential. Being able to find gainful employment or stable housing, for instance, is significantly more difficult with a criminal record than with a juvenile record that can be expunged (Pager 2003). Such a complex cost-benefit analysis has yet to be undertaken. It is therefore impossible to cast a definitive judgment on the actual efficacy of holding juveniles in the adult prison system. Negative effects may be difficult to pin down in comparison to juvenile adjudication. Yet, neither can we point to long-term positive results.

CONCLUSION

Today the "super-predator" argument has run its course. According to the Office of Juvenile Justice and Delinquency Prevention, juvenile crime has fallen to historic lows.[12] Dilulio himself retracted his theory in 2001. "If I knew then what I know now," he told a *New York Times* reporter, "I would have shouted for prevention of crimes" (Becker 2001). In 2016 Hillary Clinton followed suit. During a private fundraiser in the early days of her campaign, a young black woman interrupted the event by holding up a sign referencing one of Clinton's quotes from the mid-1990s: "They are often the kinds of kids that are called 'super-predators,' no conscience, no empathy, we can talk about why they ended up that way, but first we have to bring them to heel." While Hillary Clinton did not apologize at the event, she later issued a written statement to the *Washington Post*, saying, "Looking back, I shouldn't have used those words, and I wouldn't use them today" (Gearan and Philip 2016). With the costs of incarceration rising, even Republicans are reconsidering their approach to crime. Lawmakers "on both sides of the aisle" have indicated their openness to so-called community sanctions where people would be supervised through probation or parole rather than incarcerated in jail or prison.[13]

While the commitment to punitive governance begins to crumble, the void left by welfare reform remains unaddressed. Given the current state of the political discourse, any relief for those who fail to find their niche in the neoliberal economy seems unlikely. In the meantime some of the young men I interviewed have already or will be reentering society soon. In prison they were protected from "cruel and unusual punishment." On the outside there is no constitutional protection against cruel and unusual poverty. After their release, there will be no social safety net that eases their transition back into a normal life. Most likely they will struggle to find jobs. Only very few will be lucky enough to find a position that pays enough to support their families. On the contrary, most will have to rely on the good graces of friends and relatives who allow them to stay on their couch for free. Being completely dependent on others will affect their self-esteem, and will make it extremely difficult for them to build a new life away from crime (Western et al. 2015; Pager 2003).

The young men that ended up at Pine Grove often missed out on even the most basic foundations of a healthy childhood and adolescents. They did not have access to nutritious food, good schools, or a safe place to live. As they came of age and were adjudicated as adults, permanent prison walls replaced the invisible boundaries that had separated them from middle-class Americans. After their release from prison their overt exclusion will again be replaced by the subtle social marginalization with which they are all too familiar. Without access to nonpunitive social services on the outside their exclusion will likely become permanent. Statistically, more than half of them will recidivate within one year post-release (Durose, Cooper, and Snyder 2014).

2. The Making of Life-Course-Persistent Offenders

Many incidences recalled by the young men during interviews went beyond ordinary childhood poverty and reached the level of traumatic experiences. The psychological impact that abuse and neglect have on young children is profound. Children who are either victimized or witness domestic violence tend to display higher levels of anger and depression (Turner, Finklehor, and Ormrod 2005). The "cycle of violence" (Spatz Widom 1989) that turns victims into victimizers manifests through a complex interaction of biological and social factors. Childhood trauma leaves a visible imprint on the young, still highly malleable brain. Chronically elevated cortisol levels, for example, may impact children's ability to adapt to stressful situations (Shonkoff et al. 2012). Experiencing childhood trauma also stunts the normal development of neural pathways and synaptic pruning—i.e., the elimination of unused synapses that takes place during early childhood and is said to continue until late adolescence. These processes determine cognitive development and may even be related to severe mental health problems such as schizophrenia that emerge during adolescence (Watt et al. 2017; Sekar et al. 2016; Selemon 2013; Feinberg 1982). The area most affected is the right brain hemisphere—the part of the brain responsible for regulating emotions and social interactions (Heide and Solomon 2006).

In this chapter I argue that childhood trauma significantly shaped the young men's criminal trajectories. Their traumatic experiences were closely related, if not caused by, their families' precarious existence. Traumas inflicted their full negative impact because the young men's families did not have easy access to nonpunitive mental health support. Thus, the absence of a social safety net not only allowed poverty to reach traumatic proportions, it also prevented diagnosis and intervention that could have mitigated destructive emotional and behavioral consequences.

Lenore Terr (1991: 11) defines trauma as an external event that leads to lasting internal changes, which can later manifest as mental illness. According to Terr's typology, Type I trauma is generated by a one-time external shock. Type II trauma results from repeated victimization and prolonged suffering. Terr uses examples from her clinical practice to illustrate the types of events she defines as traumatic; for example, death of a parent or sibling, or different types of sexual abuse and physical violence. Felitti et al.'s (1998) adverse childhood experience inventory more specifically distinguishes among psychological, physical, and sexual abuse, household dysfunction, and criminal behavior in the household.

Based on Terr's and Felitti et al.'s work, I have developed a cluster of traumatic events that recurred in the young men's narratives. I coded the interviews according to three main categories and ten subcategories: (1) Violence: being physically abused, being verbally abused, violence between parents, neighborhood violence; (2) Extreme Poverty: food scarcity, homelessness; (3) Breaking of Social Ties: death, incarceration, Department of Children and Families (DCF) involvement, other. DCF involvement indicates either that mothers voluntarily gave up custody or that the DCF intervened and placed children in care of a relative, in most cases the grandmother. The subcategory "other" subsumes cases in which mothers or fathers left their children in care of the other parent or a grandparent. In one case a mother abducted the respondent and his brother, who were in the care of their father at the time.

Eleven young men recall four or more traumatic events during their early childhood. Fourteen respondents remembered two or three traumatic experiences. Twenty respondents report that they lost a caregiver (death or incarceration were the most common reasons). Seven experienced food scarcity growing up, and three young men witnessed extreme neighborhood violence such as a friend or relative being gunned down. The most extreme cases, represented in Table 1, combined a Level 1 trauma, such as witnessing the death of a friend, with extended physical and emotional abuse and neglect.[1]

In addition to the sheer number of traumatic life events, the intersection between Level 1 and Level 2 trauma in this group of respondents is notable. Abject poverty, the "prolonged suffering" (Terr 1991) of the young men and their families, created the conditions under which Level 1 traumas are more prone to take place and are less likely to be managed therapeutically later on. Living in a poor urban neighborhood, for example, increases the likelihood that a child witnesses gun violence, especially in cases where family members are involved in gangs. These families likely also do not

TABLE 2: High Level of Childhood Trauma

Name	Race	Exposure to Violence					Extreme Poverty		Breaking Ties			
		Physical Abuse	Verbal Abuse	Domestic Violence between Parents	Death of a Friend	Neighborhood Violence	Food Scarcity	Housing insecurity	Death of Caregiver	Incarceration of Caregiver	DCF Involvement	Other
Bryan	Black	X		X			X					X
Connor	Mixed	X		X				X	X			
Dylan	Black	X	X	X	X	X				X		
Gabriel	Black				X	X	X	X				
Henry	White	X	X	X					X			
Jesus	Latino	X		X	X	X						
Jordan	Black	X	X	X						X		
Joshua	Black	X		X			X				X	
Luke	White	X		X					X			
Miguel	Latino			X			X	X	X			X
Tyler	Black	X	X									

TABLE 3: Medium Level of Childhood Trauma

| | | Exposure to Violence | | | | | Extreme Poverty | | Breaking Ties | | | |
| | | | | Domestic Violence between | Death of a | Neighborhood | Food | Housing | Death of | Incarceration | DCF | |
Name	Race	Physical Abuse	Verbal Abuse	Parents	Friend	Violence	Scarcity	insecurity	Caregiver	of Caregiver	Involvement	Other
Alexander	Latino	X					X		X			
Andrew	Mixed			X							X	
Blake	Black					X				X		
Isaac	Black					X				X		
Jaxon	Black						X	X				
Jeremiah	Black			X							X	
Julian	White		X	X						X		
Kayden	Black					X						X
Marc	Black						X	X				X
Mateo	Latino			X								
Nate	Asian	X		X								
Robert	White								X	X		
William	White											X

TABLE 4: Low Level of Childhood Trauma

Name	Race	Exposure to Violence					Extreme Poverty			Breaking Ties		
		Physical Abuse	Verbal Abuse	Domestic Violence between Parents	Death of a Friend	Neighborhood Violence	Food Scarcity	Housing insecurity	Death of Caregiver	Incarceration of Caregiver	DCF Involvement	Other
Austin	Black		X									
Elijah	Black			X								
John	Mixed					X						
Josiah	Black			X								
Oliver	White											X
Samuel	Black											

have the financial means to pay for effective, individualized therapeutic interventions in the aftermath of a traumatic event.

The narratives affirm that most respondents have been severely traumatized during their childhood. A great majority had not previously opened up about their experiences.[2] When I asked them why they never told anyone about their home life before, the answer usually was that they would not have felt comfortable sharing that information with a representative of the criminal or juvenile justice system—even if that person was a therapist or social worker. The young men's mental health problems remained below the surface, even though they participated in a variety of juvenile justice interventions. Consequently, the unaddressed trauma could fully unfold its negative impact on their decision-making skills, impulse control, and general emotional well-being.

LIFE-COURSE-PERSISTENT OFFENDERS

Terrie Moffitt's (1993) taxonomy of life-course-persistent versus adolescence-limited offenders offers further insight into the relationship between childhood adversity and persistent antisocial behavior. Moffitt argues that a majority of offenders will age out of crime some time after adolescence. Adolescence-limited offending is driven by a "maturity gap." Teenagers turn to deviance when their physical development has already reached maturity while they are still considered children socially. Life-course-persistent offenders, in contrast, begin to display antisocial behavior during early childhood and continue offending past adolescence.

According to Moffitt, life-course-persistent offending has its roots in an adverse early childhood environment. Maternal drug use and general poor prenatal care, for example, disrupt neural growth. When newborns are emotionally neglected, insufficiently stimulated, and lack access to nutritious food, they experience delays in executive functions and verbal abilities. As Moffitt points out, "the link between neuropsychological impairment and antisocial outcomes is one of the most robust effects in the study of antisocial behavior" (680). While the relationship between antisocial behavior and neuropsychological deficits operates independently of class, "children with cognitive and temperamental disadvantage are generally not born into supportive environments" (681). Parents, whose children suffer from neuropsychological impairment, tend to be cognitively challenged themselves. They have neither the economic nor social capital to advocate for their children. As a result, the families who need it most often lack access to the kind of interventions that would allow their children to catch up to their peers over time (ibid.).

A great majority of the young men in this study grew up in families unable to care for them adequately when they were infants or toddlers. The PADOC files offer several data points in support of the life-course-persistent offender paradigm. A majority of the respondents, for instance, had below-average IQ scores. PADOC reports IQ scores for twenty-one of thirty respondents. Those scores range between 75 and 120. Three respondents measure over 100 (the average IQ in the population), whereas ten score between 75 and 89, and five of those ten score less than 80, a threshold that conventionally indicates borderline intellectual functioning. Koenen et al. (2007) find that low IQ is a risk factor for developing PTSD, in that a low IQ might limit someone's ability to narrativize and work through traumatic experiences. The below-average IQ of most respondents therefore constitutes a disadvantage. Not only are the young men more likely to experience trauma, their low IQ scores may also predispose them to developing PTSD.

The young men's case summary files also testify to limited educational achievement and their early onset of violent offending. Both aspects are factored into the Pennsylvania Risk Screen Tool (RST) that is administered to every inmate held at a state correctional institution. RST scores range from 0 to 9 with a higher number indicating a higher risk of recidivism. The average RST score for this group was 5.8 and is slightly higher than the 5.4 average my colleagues and I calculated based on a full sample of PADOC prisoners (Soyer et al. 2017). Two-thirds of the respondents have RST scores of 6 or 7.[3]

Both IQ and RST scores are quantifiable indicators that the young men grew up in socially and economically deprived social environments. Beyond these standardized measurements, the PADOC files do not include any valuable information about the specific abuse and neglect the respondents experienced. To understand the level of adversity the young men lived through, it is necessary to delve deeper into the narrative data.

CHILDHOOD POVERTY AND VIOLENCE

According to his case summary file Joshua is nineteen years old, African American, and six feet tall. He has brown eyes and weighs 190 pounds. Joshua was seventeen when he was charged as an adult for robbery. His social history states that he denies "any form of childhood abuse." The file also notes that Joshua insists "his basic needs were met" when he was growing up. In the interviews Joshua and his mother offer a very different narrative. His mother, a former crack addict, readily admits to her parenting failures. She recalls that Joshua's father was abusive, beating her and controlling her social life. When she was pregnant with Joshua, she left her partner only to start dating another abusive man. "I been through hell and back and my kids [have] been there with me," she says.

Her parenting choices reflect the domestic violence that she herself endured. She remembers almost choking "the life out [of]" her son when Joshua was eight years old. It was her way of punishing him for stealing money from her. As I speak to her eleven years later, she expresses remorse about this incident. After she had gone for her son's throat, she called the police herself, telling the dispatcher: "I'm gonna need you to come get him before I kill him." When the police saw the red marks on Joshua's neck, he ended up in foster care. Joshua, however, wanted to stay with his mother. He ran away from different foster care placements, just to show up at her doorstep again. As she puts it: "So every day, Joshua would be here [with me]. No matter where they took Joshua, no matter what facility they took him, he brought his ass right back here."

Although Joshua loves his mother, he struggles to recover happy childhood memories. There were too many siblings and other relatives who needed to be taken care of and not enough resources for everybody. Access to nutritious food wasn't anything that he could take for granted. "Ramen noodles—that was lunch, dinner, and sometimes breakfast," he remembers. And occasionally there were not even ramen noodles to be had. On those days, he fought hunger pains: "You feel like your stomach is touching your back, your head hurt, and then, it would always be physically." When he was younger, Joshua used to be angry about the poverty and instability he confronted on a daily basis: "I wanted a normal [life], to be able to have a conversation with somebody else and we talk about family, you know, good memories, . . . and have fun pictures from when you was younger. I didn't have none of that."

This intersection between poverty, drugs, and violence particularly impacted the young men who grew up in urban areas. Jesus, a twenty-year-old Latino man from Kensington, Philadelphia, describes the general despair he witnessed in his neighborhood:

> You see a lot of weird shit, like being around fiends all day. We called it the walking dead down there, 'cause all you see is fiends, doped out, cracked out, walking slow. Like, like they're dead. . . . You might walk by and you see a fiend overdosing on their arm, or they already overdosed. . . . Or you'd be chilling and somebody would be shooting at the block over 'cause they want their money or drugs. Or next block you might be around and somebody catch a stray bullet. Or over at basketball game, somebody get shot.

Gabriel, who spent some of his childhood in Pittsburgh, witnessed the murder of his friend on a playground next to the shelter where he was staying at the time with his mother and siblings:

> This is when I was in like fourth or fifth grade. . . . Like you'd be so young, you'd be so not thinking, you just hear the noise. . . . I remember he was by the slide, and then I came down by him on the slide and he was just lying there. I think it hit his chest or something like that. I went downstairs, and his mom's yelling, screaming, everybody's screaming and all that.

Jesus remembers a similar incident:

> My cousin got killed in front of me. And, we was all around. . . . It all started over a fight. . . . It was a summer day, everybody was around. And two bulls [physically strong males] came walking on the street, but they got hoodies on. We like, what the hell is going on? We thinking they were smokers, like fiends. Bull just walked up to my cousin, and just shoot him in his head. I'm like, what the hell? I see his body drop, and my grandmom scream, everybody screamed. Ahh, what's going on? Know what I'm saying? These two running off. Like oh shit, shit real. This was before I even really, really took the streets serious. I was like 10 or 11. I started having problems, like I was messed up. I went to [the] crazy hospital like a week after that. I wanted to kill my teacher. I was mad at everybody. . . . I was pretty messed up for a little bit.

Even though Jesus recalls that he spent time in a psychiatric hospital, the violence he witnessed was quickly buried under the constant struggle that engulfed his childhood.

Like Jesus, Alexander grew up in an area where hearing gunshots was a daily occurrence. Amidst the general violence, Alexander also was an eyewitness to his aunt's murder:

> I was in the room with my aunt when this happened. I was in the room with my aunt, and they got into an argument. He shot her. Just pulled the gun out, they was arguing and I was watching them. He shot her and ran out the door. My uncles started chasing him. The cops caught him and killed him 'cause the cops surrounded him, and he started shooting at the cops. And then, the cops shot him.

At the time of our interview Alexander still recalls PTSD-like symptoms that started after he witnessed his aunt's violent death: "I'd wake up sweating all the time . . . I always wake up and be all shakin' and stuff." He never saw a psychiatrist and initially believed that waking up shaking and sweating may be an aspect of hitting puberty. After a while getting shot at also became an occupational hazard of his gang involvement. Alexander lost two more friends to gun violence.

Most of the white respondents, who lived in rural or suburban areas, confronted less violence on the neighborhood level. Their life histories are nevertheless interspersed with personal tragedies and deprivation. Henry, for example, grew up in a small town close to Pittsburgh. He is over six feet tall with short-cropped, blond hair. His arms and neck are covered in tattoos. Henry's parents divorced soon after he was born. Each of them remarried and Henry moved back and forth between his father and mother. The brief social history in his file indicates "no substance abuse or domestic violence among his family members." In our interviews Henry remembers a much more volatile childhood. His father, who was an alcoholic, initially received custody because of his mother's drug addiction. Henry was placed in foster care when his father showed up at his school drunk and threatened to "punch his son in the face." Henry hated his foster care placement and went on the run shortly after he had arrived there.

Despite his father's alcoholism, he preferred to stay with him rather than with his mother and stepfather. Henry vividly remembers that his stepfather physically and emotionally abused him as a young child:

I can remember, I might have been like five, it was like 1999 or early 2000. . . . I'm down there and my mom she gave me two lollipops. And she said, here, you can have them after dinner, and she went to work. She worked until like three in the morning. So after I get done with dinner, I go . . . they're on top of the fridge, so I climb up there and get them. My stepdad gets mad because I didn't ask him. But my mom already told me I could have them. So he takes them and puts them back up there, I throw a little fit. He locks me in the bathroom, dark, and any time I turn the light on; he come in there and whoop my ass. [He] made me stay in the dark that whole night until about one in the morning before my mom came home.

Robert, another white participant, also grew up in a small town. His mother was an alcoholic and had been arrested for DUIs multiple times. Robert remembers drunken fights between his parents but can no longer recall the details. At seven years old, Robert lost his father to suicide. When his father shot himself at a gun range, his mother was serving twenty-three months in county jail for drunk driving. He remembers feeling like both of his parents had abandoned him. After his father's death, Robert lived with his grandmother, his father's mother. She was in her late sixties when I visited her. The small, crumbling house used to belong to her parents. She had lived in it all her life and it was the only property she had ever owned. A few years ago her daughter bought the house to avoid foreclosure.

The poverty of Robert and his family symbolizes the decline of the white, rural working class. Fifty years ago, when Robert's grandmother came of age, Robert's hometown was prosperous. His great-grandfather and his grandfather worked for Bethlehem Steel. Back then, his grandmother remembers, the rumbling from the train tracks by her house never stopped. Today the tracks are eerily quiet. According to Robert's grandmother, "everything went to the dogs" when the steel mills closed. By the time Robert was a teenager, those who could leave had left. The white, working-class part of the town that Robert and his family live in turned into a predominantly African American neighborhood. As Robert's family was struggling to hold on to the little they had, helping Robert to cope with the loss of his father was a low priority. As Robert's grandmother remembers, her daughter-in-law simply expected Robert to "get over it."

THE SOCIAL ORIGIN OF MALFORMED HABITS

The above narratives indicate that Level 1 and Level 2 traumas are intertwined in the young men's experience. The traumatic incidences that fall into the Level 1 category are framed by the abject poverty and generalized violence—the Level II trauma—that defined their lives. Middle-class children may also experience traumatic events; however, their trauma is more likely to be an isolated event rather than a constant experience of deprivation and violence.

Acknowledging that the young men in this book lived through a traumatic childhood is the first step toward humanizing inmates who have been stigmatized as incorrigible "super-predators." The neuropsychological lens is indispensable for understanding pathways into crime. On the other hand, framing criminality as a social problem of the uneducated, cognitively challenged underclass allows the majority to absolve themselves from any responsibility toward those who have shown to be "unfit" for living a middle-class lifestyle for generations.[4]

The social philosopher John Dewey offers an important perspective on the responsibility of society as a whole for individual criminal acts. Taking his view seriously, I believe, allows for an analysis of pathological behavior but without blaming the individual for his or her moral failings. Dewey's understanding of socialization and identity development argues that society—in this case American society, not just the immediate family or peer networks—bears responsibility for the criminal acts the young men committed.

In *Human Nature and Conduct* Dewey develops a theory of identity and habit formation that is fundamentally social in its approach. Dewey sees habits as a form of action and argues that they are acquired through interaction with the social environment. Habits, as he puts it, "involve the support of environing conditions" ([1922] 1988: 16). Any action we engage in is a shared endeavor. The response a specific conduct elicits from the surrounding environment invariably shapes an actor's future behavior. According to Dewey, it is therefore impossible to separate human conduct from the social environment in which the individual is embedded.[5]

Dewey's ideas are especially important for understanding the emergence of criminal behavior. Rejecting a metaphysical understanding of morality, Dewey proposes that good and bad behaviors are established through adaptation to the environment. "Punitive justice," he argues, fails to recognize the "social partnership in producing crime" (ibid., 17). Assuming a "social partnership," however, does not imply that human beings are pure products of their environment. The social environment and the individual are inseparable from each other and they both influence habit formation.

I refer to Dewey's work because, more than other theorists, he emphasizes the social nature of action. According to Dewey, similar habits develop because people react to the same set of circumstances in almost identical ways. Likewise, morals that guide individual behavior emerge out of the group. "Each person," Dewey argues, "is born an infant, and every infant is subject from the first breath he draws and the first cry he utters to the attention and demands of others" (ibid.).

Taking Dewey's perspective to its logical conclusion implies that criminal behavior is a form of social action for which both parties, the individual and society, bear responsibility. Individual behavior manifests itself as a reaction to values that go beyond the individual family unit, or even local institutions.

Following Dewey, the young men's criminal behavior should be understood as malformed habits. These habits are formed in relation to the different social structures in which they are embedded. Gabriel, the young man from Pittsburgh, spent his childhood moving between shelters in violent neighborhoods. He developed his habits in relation to this volatile environment. His mother, who was still a child herself when Gabriel was born, was also adapting to these challenging circumstances. While Gabriel and his mother were able to exercise agency, the choices in front of them were limited and more likely to lead down a criminal path (McLeod 2008).

Dewey's ideas seem to contradict the core American value of individualism. Yet even John Stuart Mill realizes that the vulnerable, not yet fully formed person deserves protection. Mill argues that the individual is sovereign "over his own body and mind." Yet he qualifies this statement by stating: "It is, perhaps, hardly necessary to say that this doctrine is meant to apply to human beings in the maturity of their faculties. We are not speaking of children or of young persons below the age which the law may fix as that of manhood or womanhood" ([1869] 1978: 9). Further he notes: "Those who are still in a state to require to be taken care of by others must be protected against their own actions as well as against external injury" (ibid.).

As children, the respondents needed protection from their own actions. By refusing to adequately support their families, American society has deprived them of their ability to live the kind of individualism American society holds dear. Mill emphasizes that "a true freedom does not attempt to deprive others of theirs or impede their efforts to obtain it" (ibid., 12). By letting poverty and trauma warp the life of these young men so fundamentally, American society is not only guilty of depriving them of freedom but also of teaching them self-destructive habits.

Focusing on the role of drug dealers in poor urban neighborhoods further exemplifies how negative habits emerge through social adaptation. While selling drugs to their mothers, several young men remember that dealers relieved their conscience by giving food and money to the children who were left uncared for. Even at a young age most of the young men understood that drug dealing is a crime. They witnessed the devastating effects that drug use had on their mothers and fathers. Nevertheless, the dealers supported them consistently in ways no other social institution did. Knowing that drug dealing is an illegal and violent trade was outweighed by the immediate gratification of having money in your pocket and by feeling a sense of belonging.

From Dewey's perspective, actors—in this case the young men—did not make a conscious choice to maximize their utility when they committed a crime. Rather, their social environment was structured such that it rewarded certain habits and discouraged others. The young men were not only desensitized to violence but also learned that neither their mothers nor the social institutions they were embedded in met their emotional and physical needs.

Acknowledging that our habits are a product of the social environment we live in does not mean absolving actors from their responsibility. Social processes are highly contingent, and human beings retain agency even under the most oppressive circumstances (Rhodes 2004). The respondents' life-course histories nevertheless raise the question of social responsibility and the need to redistribute wealth. With more comprehensive support for young single mothers, Joshua's mother may have felt empowered to leave her abusive spouses much earlier. Access to mental health services may have diagnosed Robert's father as suicidal in time for him to receive psychological help. Speculating about these potentialities reveals the extent to which American society has abandoned any concept of shared responsibility for the well-being of those who are—at least momentarily—unable to take care of themselves.

CONCLUSION

The young men I interviewed represent the tail end of the poverty and violence distribution—even in disadvantaged communities. They had long criminal histories and dealt with an unusual amount of trauma in their lives. These young men are "life-course-persistent offenders"—a small fraction of the population that is responsible for a large volume of criminal behavior (Moffitt 1993). Their long-term involvement in the criminal justice system has been costly, even without counting the lost human capital.

Given the clear connection between childhood trauma and criminal behavior, researchers have long advocated for systematic, better-suited mental health services in the juvenile justice system (Ford et al. 2012; Teplin et al. 2002). In 2012, Attorney General Eric Holder's National Task Force on Children Exposed to Violence elevated the prevalence of childhood trauma to an issue of national importance. The task force's executive summary argues that millions of American children experience or witness violence and abuse. Children in the juvenile justice system, the report maintains, have "almost always been exposed to several types of violence" (Listenbee et al. 2012: 171). Therefore, "integrating widely available and culturally adaptive interventions for traumatized children . . . in the juvenile justice system" is an absolute necessity (180).

Despite this call for action, treatment of childhood trauma has not been systemically integrated in juvenile justice interventions. Most importantly, even the task force's critical accounting overlooks the crucial relationship between childhood trauma and abject poverty that is clearly visible in the data I have collected.

According to the National Center for Children in Poverty at Columbia University, in 2016, 23 percent of infants and toddlers under the age of three live in families that make less than the federal poverty threshold (Jian, Granja, and Koball 2017). So far, American society has not taken responsibility for the high level of childhood poverty in its midst. Extreme poverty creates the backdrop of a social environment in which children are victimized by overwhelmed caregivers and dysfunctional social institutions. By neglecting poverty as a catalyst for trauma, it is still possible to blame parents for failing to raise their children adequately.

John Dewey, on the other hand, describes criminal behavior as a shared social act. For him any action is social because the principles that guide our decision-making are inseparable from the society we live in. The trauma the young men lived through is rooted in their families' marginalized social position. Their choices are *not* just a reaction to specific pressures (Agnew 1992). Better coping skills or higher self-esteem could not have protected them from hunger pains. Their criminal behavior manifested in relation to a dysfunctional social structure that has brutally cast aside those unable to succeed in a globalized economy.

Over the last three decades the United States has progressively dismantled social welfare for its poorest citizens. The respondents had to cope with extreme poverty and violence that put them at an almost insurmountable disadvantage. Even under the best of circumstances the trauma they lived through can create irreparable psychological damage and behavioral problems. Poor families do not receive high-quality psychological support. In fact, nonpunitive treatment options are not easily accessible for most of them (Soyer 2016). As a result, the trauma that interrupted the respondents' childhood was never addressed and eventually forgotten amidst the daily struggle of making ends meet.

In the chapters that follow I focus on the specific ways childhood trauma, poverty, and crime are interwoven in the life-course histories of the young men. The respondents used criminal behavior to create the illusion of agency over an environment that was beyond their control. Many had become desensitized to violence, and they could barely imagine how their lives might have been if their childhood had not been defined by a lack of food, shelter, and clothing.

3. The End of Childhood

Parental Drug Addiction and Violence

When a child between ages fifteen and eighteen is charged with an Act 33 offense, he "does not meet the [Pennsylvania] Juvenile Act definition of a child."[1] The Department of Corrections does not have to seek parental consent for medical treatment. The parents also do not have to give permission for their child's participation in research.[2] While the childhoods of the young men in this study "officially" ended when they were adjudicated as adults, many had been taking on adult roles long before they legally ceased to be children.

In this chapter I focus on the young men's traumatic experiences that are related to parental drug addiction. Parents' drug-seeking behaviors created a reversed version of the "maturity gap" that Moffitt (1993) observed in adolescence-limited offenders. When parents were unable to take care of their children's basic needs, the respondents had to take over social roles requiring foresight and independent decision-making well beyond their cognitive capacity. While still biologically children, their social environment expected them to take on adult social roles. This role reversal between parents and children made it very difficult for juvenile justice interventions to have a meaningful effect on the young men. The programs did not address the trauma they had lived through, nor did the rehabilitative efforts take into account that the youth had been taking care of themselves and their siblings for years and thus struggled with accepting adult authority of any kind.

Children who grow up poor face many existential hardships unknown to middle-class children. They are confronted with their parents' inability to provide emotional and financial stability (Desmond 2016; Edin and Shaefer 2015). The current opioid epidemic shows that drug dependency can cross class, race, and gender boundaries. The fallout of parental drug addiction, however, differentially impacts children living in poverty. Dealing with their parents' substance abuse was especially difficult for the African American respondents who grew up in areas of concentrated poverty. Their families lacked the social and economic capital to treat drug addiction and to shield children from the consequences of their parents' drug-seeking behaviors. Children who lived with drug-addicted caretakers faced housing insecurity, food scarcity, and loss of a caregiver, as well as physical and verbal abuse on a daily basis.[3]

For a majority of the respondents, parental drug or alcohol dependency exacerbated their already marginal existence. The absence of any form of government support that could compensate for the individual lack of economic resources and supportive social ties made it almost impossible for the young men to escape the cycle of violence and crime that parental addiction generated.

MATURITY GAP AND PARENTAL DRUG ADDICTION

Table 5 shows that twenty out of the thirty respondents had drug-addicted parents. Ten cases involved maternal or paternal addiction to crack or heroin. Seven respondents grew up in families where either fathers or mothers were dependent on alcohol. Five respondents reported that one or both parents struggled with alcohol abuse and also were addicted to crack or heroin. One remembered his father smoking marijuana regularly. In three cases, the type of parental drug addiction was not specified. Only ten of the thirty respondents did not explicitly mention that their parents had any substance-abuse issues.[4]

Parental drug addiction overlapped significantly with experiencing a high level of childhood trauma. Nine respondents who reported parental drug addiction also fall into the "High Level of Childhood Trauma" category (see earlier Table 2). Put differently, only two out of the eleven young men who have lived through a high level of childhood trauma *did not* report parental drug addiction. The exact opposite is the case for the young men in the low-level trauma category. Only two out of the six respondents in this group indicated that their parents struggled with substance abuse. Respondents growing up with parents addicted to drugs were much more likely to live through several traumatic incidents.

According to the 2013 National Survey on Drug Use and Health (NSDUH) 3.6 percent of the U.S. population used illicit drugs other than marijuana.[5] In comparison to this small percentage of illicit drug users in the total population, parental drug use is vastly overrepresented in this group of young men. This overrepresentation becomes meaningful when we analyze

TABLE 5: Parental Drug Addiction

	Crack	Alcohol	Heroin	Marijuana	Unspecified
Andrew	X				
Austin		X			
Bryan*		X		X	
Connor*		X			
Dylan*	X	X			
Gabriel*	X				
Henry*		X			
Jeremiah	X				
Jordan*	X			X	
Joshua*	X				
Josiah					X
Julian	X	X			
Kayden				X	
Luke*		X	X		
Marc					X
Miguel*		X			
Nate		X			
Oliver	X	X			
Robert		X			
William		X			

NOTE: The self-reported data is inevitably incomplete. The young men who did not report any parental drug addiction may not have been willing or emotionally capable of sharing this likely painful part of their childhood with me. For further elaboration on methodological limitations, see Appendix I, "Metholodical Reflections." Respondents fall into the High Level of Childhood Trauma category.

how parental drug addiction impacted the respondents' pathways into crime. Those who had drug-addicted parents were more likely to experience extreme economic hardship or the loss of a caregiver. Parental drug consumption opened up opportunities for crime. Children of drug-addicted parents had a lot of unsupervised time to themselves. They spent less time at home and more time around their friends to avoid the consequences of their parents' erratic behavior. In cases where caregivers financed their drug habit with drug dealing, the young men easily became part of their parents' business. Some even recall that they served as their parents' dealer.

Drug-addicted parents, more than other caregivers in this study, failed to fulfill their children's basic needs. Those who grew up in households dominated by substance abuse cite extreme resource deprivation as a justification for their initial petty crimes (Sykes and Matza 1957). Finally, when parents were incapacitated, it was left to the children to figure out how to take care of younger siblings, what to do if there was no food in the fridge, and how to pay the bills. Being forced into adult roles created a false sense of autonomy. Once the respondents entered puberty, misconceptions about their status within the family and larger society had already taken root. They continued to overestimate their decision-making capacity and became immune to parental or juvenile justice interventions. The respondents faced an acute maturity gap. Moffitt (1993) argues that adolescence-limited offenders have reached biological maturity but are not yet considered adults by their social environment. The young men I interviewed, in contrast, had to function as adults even before they reached puberty. Biologically they were still children, yet their social environment left them no choice but to take on adult responsibilities.

CONCENTRATED DISADVANTAGE

Analyzing four brief case studies of African American respondents demonstrates the enduring significance of racial segregation. While all of the respondents came from disadvantaged families, the African American youths faced a particular set of hardships. They lived in racially segregated neighborhoods that lacked institutional resources. Their narratives expose that poverty exacerbated by parental drug addictions hit African American youths even more profoundly than the white and Latino men I interviewed. Even though the six white respondents grew up with parents who were addicted to either drugs or alcohol, a modicum of social and economic capital shielded them from the desperation and extreme poverty the African American youths recalled (Desmond 2016; Massey and Denton 1993; Wilson 1990).

"I got the really shitty end of the stick"

Dylan grew up in a house with his mother, his aunt, and a total of eleven other children. He never had a bed to sleep in when he was a child. His mother was addicted to crack and his stepfather was a violent alcoholic. Shame related to his parents' behaviors is one of his predominant childhood memories: "Like your own mom sucking dick and shit like that. And niggas know that you over here, mom sucking dick for work. My mom out there fucking getting high. I got to deal with that growing up," he remembers.

His stepfather was a violent man but he particularly took his anger out on Dylan. "I got the real shitty end of the stick," he says. Dylan believes his stepfather hurt him more than the other children because he was the only one of the siblings who was not his biological child. Dylan's mother was in a relationship with another man while his stepfather was incarcerated. As Dylan puts it: "While he was locked up, he told my mom she could fuck other niggas. And my mom fucked other niggas, so she had a baby and he got mad."

When Dylan's mother stopped smoking crack, she replaced her drug habit with pills and began selling oxycodone. Dylan became part of her dealings. At the time he was already selling marijuana. They found a doctor willing to write prescriptions for painkillers in exchange for Dylan's marijuana and some additional payment.

Between the ages of thirteen and sixteen, before Dylan was arrested for third-degree murder, he had no stable place to live. Back then he was heavily involved in street life and mostly slept on other people's couches. He claims that he still gave his mother $400 per month to help her with her $750 rent check. Dylan says he did not know that there was any other way to live. "I don't even think I knew foster families existed back then. I don't even think that shit was in my mind," he explains. Growing up around a lot of violence and drug consumption, he believes, desensitized him: "When I feel like I'm angry or end up fighting, I be taking shit to the extreme . . . . Like the average shit that scares somebody else wouldn't scare me." While he seems to understand that taking another person's life is wrong, he also says he did not feel remorse when he was adjudicated: "I'm not about to sit here in court and cry 'cause a nigga try to kill me and I got him first," he says. He likes to see himself as a soldier who hurts enemies in combat. He says he never knew any other way to be:

> I don't got no man growing up. I got my daddy, out hauling, he never there. Then, I got my step-pop who just whoop my ass. So, where am I supposed to find a guy that I can follow? My brother? . . . My brother he was locked up from the time he was twelve. Beat it. That's what I had to follow.

Children like Dylan should be considered victims of the crack epidemic that wreaked havoc in American inner cities during the mid-1980s and early 1990s (Contreras 2013). While Dylan did not smoke crack himself, the destructive impact that crack had on the social fabric surrounding him shaped his early childhood. Dylan's case exemplifies that social problems as extreme as the crack epidemic cause persistent trauma across generations. Historians and sociologists have observed that children born to parents who have lived through war and displacement suffer a form of second-generation trauma (Epstein 1979; Yehuda et al. 2001). The same very likely holds true to children born during the crack era. A whole generation of children whose parents were addicted to crack may have been scarred by the drug's destructive fallout for the rest of their lives.

"If I needed something, I'd do it myself"

Addiction and dealing drugs were part of Jordan's life for as long as he can remember. Guns where hidden under the sofa where he used to sleep. People sneaked in and out of his house to avoid the police, and gunshots were coming through the window. Similar to Dylan, Jordan also did not have a relationship with his father. His father, a crack addict, never stayed out of rehab or jail long enough to be a part of his life. "I didn't really have no father figure," he says. The "old heads" of the neighborhood looked after him instead. Jordan's mother was never a steady presence in his life either. She was in a violent and volatile relationship with another man. Jordan remembers that she struggled to get by and he learned quickly that he had to find a way to get what he needed. From his perspective, selling drugs was the only way he could take care of himself when his mother didn't: "Everybody going to school with clean clothes on, clean sneaks, and you ain't got that so you know you can hustle and get it," he explains.

In 2005, when his father went back to jail, one of the old heads took Jordan under his wing. As he tells it, his life got a lot better then: "He was buying me clothes, I was selling drugs, I was staying at his house, was getting girls. He was making sure I was going to school with the newest sneakers and fresh to death. And I liked that."

Turning the mother-son relationship completely on its head, Jordan recalls that his mother stole the money he made dealing drugs. He had always been the most important source of income for the family. His mother made him "act crazy," engaging in repetitive and disruptive behavior so that he would become eligible for Social Security payments. His brother, Jordan recalls, didn't do as good as a job as he did acting out in front of the psychologists who were supposed to evaluate him. When I ask him if his mother ever took care of him, he replies:

> If I had, if ya'll could just sit here and play my past back . . . you'd probably cry. 'Cause it came to a point where I used to really just do dirty shit. Like if I was thirsty, we had water and shit. But the house was so dirty, like roaches and rats, mouses. . . . I used to just do dumb stuff. Like put a T-bone steak, a big ass steak, in the microwave. So hungry, [I] eat that shit cold. And shit like that, just to eat and steal. Go to the neighbor's house and steal.

By the time he was thirteen, his mother had lost any authority over him. When she tried to discipline him for getting suspended from school he remembers telling her: "You don't buy me shit, I do everything myself. You don't wake me up for school. You don't cook me breakfast. You don't buy my clothes. You don't do that. I do that myself. I'm not gonna let you beat me." He couldn't even rely on her helping him to reenroll in school after he had been expelled: "If I needed something, I'd do it myself."

Right before he was caught for the robbery that sent him to Pine Grove, he stayed with a neighbor, who became as close to a mother figure as he ever had. His mother had hung up the phone before hearing me out, but I was able to track Ms. Taneesha down, as Jordan calls her. When I speak to the woman Jordan considers a mother-like friend, I realize that she knows very little about him. One of her sons used to be in Pine Grove as well and another one just got arrested. She has her own children to worry about.

Ms. Taneesha remembers that Jordan's mother was never around: "She never put him first. It was always her men [she put first]," she says. Especially after both his mother and father were incarcerated, Jordan was on his own. By the time he was on his juvenile probation, he was immune to any adult intervention. When his probation officer tried to prevent him from hanging out with older guys, he simply told her "to shut up."

Jordan was one year and a few months shy of being parole eligible when I met him. His case summary file states that he plans to live with his father once he is released. All he wants to do, however, is to take care of his mother. During our last interview, I asked him why he is not angry with her for all she put him through. He explains that he never knew anything different. By the time he realized the extent of his mother's dysfunctional behavior, he just accepted it: "By then," he says, "it was already like, fuck it. Like I'm already here." Almost paradoxically, Jordan feels responsible for his mother even today. He says he loves his mother "to death" and he always wanted to give her "everything she needs": clothes, money, respect, all the things she didn't get from the men in her life.

Jordan's narrative demonstrates the reverse "maturity gap" that especially plagued respondents growing up with drug-addicted parents. Still a child in the biological, legal, and cognitive sense, Jordan could not take care of himself. He was too young to be legally employed. He did not even know how to cook food or how to wash his clothes and haphazardly bridged the gap between his legal age and his social responsibilities by committing crimes.

"I hated living in shelters"

Gabriel, a young black man who grew up in Pittsburgh, remembers "a lot of pain" when he thinks about his childhood. Gabriel's family had to survive on very few resources. He remembers living in a home with ten people: eight children (his cousins and brothers) and two adults (his mother and aunt). As he moved between homeless and battered-women shelters, there was never enough money to cover even the most basic expenses. He remembers being angry at his mother for not being able to find a stable place to live: "When I was young I used to be mad, because we used to live in shelters and stuff and I hated living in shelters, so bad, and my mom used to always have us in shelters." It was at one of these shelters that Gabriel's friend was killed by a stray bullet right in front of him as both of them were playing on a nearby playground.[6]

Gabriel's mother gave birth to him when she was fifteen years old. Still a child herself she failed to take on a maternal role. Gabriel remembers that she was never at home. It was Gabriel's responsibility to take care of his younger siblings, get them dressed, and take them to school. Gabriel himself went to school only irregularly. Without his mother there, he had a lot of freedom. He could go out whenever he wanted and come back home as late as he wanted. In the morning he was often too tired to go to school himself. He enjoyed having that much autonomy though, and it was difficult for him to accept his mother's authority once she became clean and tried to assert herself again as a caregiver.

Gabriel started selling drugs when he was around eleven years old. He began his career as a lookout for other dealers. A few years later he graduated to selling weed and eventually moved on to crack and cocaine. His mother was an important gateway into the drug business. Gabriel watched her selling cocaine to finance her own consumption. When Gabriel began selling, he eventually became his mother's supplier.

Gabriel's brother is also incarcerated at Pine Grove. He was sent there after Gabriel, and at the time of the interview he stayed in one of the transitionary housing units that are part of the prison as well. I was able to interview him, and like Gabriel, he has very few joyful memories of their childhood. He remembers that being poor and hungry played a big part in why he was drawn to the streets. He tries to be empathetic about his mother's situation. Yet, he also admits that he cannot understand why she did not put her kids first. "I would do what's best for my kids. . . . I just felt like she did what's best for herself a lot of the time," he says.

In the end, the drug dealers on the corner did for Gabriel what his mother couldn't do: "I know it's cliché," he explains, "but people selling drugs probably took care of us more than my mom when I was young. Give us money, do stuff." He remembers people in fancy cars giving him money:

"They see you messed up, dirty, wearing the same clothes, out all day . . . so, they know what type of situation you're in."

When Gabriel was a teenager his mother's cocaine addiction spiraled out of control. During that time she barely came home. Gabriel tries to think of any happy moments from his childhood, but can't recall any: "I've never been to an amusement park, never been to a water park," he explains, adding, "I [have] only been to the zoo one time, that's when I took my son to the zoo."

Providing for his own son is a priority for him. From his perspective, it may even be worth it to be incarcerated as long as he knows that his son has access to some of the money he made from selling drugs. He explains: "I'd rather be in jail and know that my family straight than me be out there, and they be messed up, my son, be going through the same stuff I'm going through." When I asked him about his future plans, Gabriel is skeptical that he can stay away from the street after he is released. He simply does not know what he would like to do with his life after he is released: "I really wasn't no school-type person," he says. When people ask him what he wants to do with his life, he can't think of anything he would like to do. "There's probably stuff that I like, I just never been exposed to it before yet."

"Money, drugs, parties"

His mother, Bryan remembers, never had enough food in the house to feed all the children: "She and her friends had to really get together, put their food stamps and WIC [Women, Infants, and Children] checks together, so we could eat," he says. His mother also did not buy new shoes and clothes for him. Selling drugs and stealing allowed him to get what he wanted. "See," he explains, "if I want a new pair of sneakers, I'll go get them myself. I'm gonna steal 'em or I'm gonna get 'em somehow. That's how it was." It would have not crossed his mind to ask his mother for money. As he tells it, he was too young to apply for government support and too young to get a job, so "hustling" was the only way for him to make money. His mother was an alcoholic and smoked marijuana. She also had a string of abusive relationships. Bryan's father had abused his mother and he continued beating up Bryan after his parents' separation.

After he had turned two, Bryan lived with his father on and off. When Bryan was around six years old, his elementary school teachers noted scars and marks that his father's beatings had left. As a result, Bryan ended up in foster care for several years. He hated the foster system even more than being on the receiving end of his father's anger: "I didn't wanna leave. No kid wants to leave their parents even if they is abusive," he explains. He preferred living with his father even though violence was the constant drumbeat of his childhood. He recalls: "I don't like coming home and being smacked in the back of my head. . . . You hitting me, hitting me 'til you draw blood, that's corny. My pop 280, six four, I'm saying? It's not fair." Bryan says he suffers from short-term memory loss and believes that his father's and stepmother's abuse did irreparable damage to his brain. His father slammed Bryan's head against the wall. His stepmother threw him against the radiator.[7]

Bryan brought the violence he experienced at home to school. When I asked him what kind of a student he was, he replies: "I remember kicking one of my teachers, she tried to pick me up, I kicked her in the knee. So, I was difficult. Always in detention, always getting suspended." He was able to leave foster care at eight and move in with his mother. Four years later he had to go back to foster care again. His mother's new husband did not tolerate Bryan in the house and Bryan despised him as well. As Bryan tells it, he tried to protect his siblings and his mother from his stepfather's rage:

> He was a nut. Like he smacked my little brother in the face, had his whole handprint in my little brother's face. My little brother is a baby. I was trying to do something. . . . I protect my family, like my little brother, little sisters, my mom.

The cops would take too long to come anyway, he explained, so he took care of it himself. As a recipient of violence, exercising violence came easy to him. "Stuff like that was just natural," he says. When he was nine years old he started killing cats and shot birds. He even killed a dog that wouldn't stop barking with a BB gun. Drowning cats, he recalls, made him feel excited: "I don't know, just to watch it die. I would just get so excited. Same thing with like shooting a gun. Just feel the recoil and the barrel is exciting. Like it just gets me excited." During his teenage years his criminal behavior reached a new level. He committed his first armed robbery at fourteen and began selling drugs. His specialty was robbing random strangers who had just left one of the neighborhood bars:

> I used to be out like two in the morning, waiting for people to come from the bars. Just random picks. [It would] be all night, all night. Repeat, and repeat, and repeat.

At that point, he did not commit crimes anymore to feed his brothers or help out his mother. He was drawn to the lifestyle and excitement that came with committing crimes. When I ask him why he committed these violent crimes, he replies:

Money, drugs, parties. You was gonna do what you wanted to do. That's basically the freedom to do what you wanna do. Some people loved a lot of money, but I just loved freedom.

Bryan readily admits that he enjoyed being unconstrained by adult supervision. Economic pressures and opportunities for crime may have provided the first incentive for criminal behavior, but having money to spend, the freedom to get high, and most importantly feeling in charge of his own destiny propelled Bryan's criminal behavior beyond meeting his immediate needs (Katz 1988).

"I hate when somebody lies to me"

In comparison to the other African American men I met at Pine Grove, Jeremiah lived a sheltered life. When his mother was incapacitated because of her crack addiction, Jeremiah's grandmother took him in. She tried to protect him as best she could from his mother's instability. Jeremiah went to Catholic school and his grandmother even arranged for him to see a therapist to deal with his mother's absence. More so than other families I met, Jeremiah's grandmother and his aunt continue to be involved in his life. Both vow to support him after his release.

Even though his family tried to compensate as best as they could for Jeremiah's mother's self-destructive behavior, her drug addiction had a devastating effect on her son: "My sister," Ms. Lewis explains, "was a horrible drug addict. She was getting high like right in our neighborhood. She was prostituting [herself] right in our neighborhood. So her children knew, they saw it." Ms. Lewis remembers her sister getting raped, getting shot at, and being beaten up by men. As she sums it up: "It's just been a horrible, horrible life for her. And a horrible life for her children because of her." Jeremiah's grandmother also believes that her daughter loves her children but lacks maternal skills and fails to prioritize her children: "If you tell her there's a party on 69th Street, she's going to that party," she explains.

Looking back at his childhood Jeremiah remembers struggling with his parents' absence and especially his mother's unreliability. Trying to find the right word, he settles on having been "confused" as a child. According to his grandmother, Jeremiah's troubles are also related to his learning disability that was handled badly at the Catholic school he attended. The new principal, his grandmother remembers, lacked compassion for children who struggled academically. When he was in seventh grade Jeremiah could only read at a third-grade level. Other kids at school and even one of the teachers made fun of him. At thirteen, trying desperately to fit in, he adapted a tough-guy street demeanor.

His aunt recalls that his transformation almost happened overnight: "I mean within six months he went from being an altar boy in private Catholic school to being a gang member. And we thought it was a joke, we're like you're not a gang member. Give me a break, there are no gangs here." Jeremiah, however, took his transformation seriously. On the day he committed the crime that led him to Pine Grove, he had originally planned to rob someone who owed him money for petty crimes he had committed on his behalf. When that plan did not materialize, he and his friends came up with a plan to rob a pizza delivery guy. The robbery got out of hand and his co-defendant stabbed the delivery man in the chest. Jeremiah was lucky. The man survived and he was only charged with aggravated assault instead of murder.

Years after Jeremiah witnessed his mother's drug abuse, he continues to be emotionally overwhelmed by the memories. He vividly recalls a moment that symbolizes his mother's carelessness and inability to keep her promises:

> We was in that house on 54th Street, right around the time when she started to come back and be with the family and started to stay around. . . . I remember her cooking some, chicken wings and potato wedges and things like that. I just remember her, matter [of] fact, she smoked crack in front of me. . . . It was something that she did that just broke me. I can't even say how I felt about when it happened, but I hate when somebody lies to me. Like you saying that you're gonna try to do your best, you saying that you're gonna be here for us, you're starting to be here for us now, and for some reason, you just do this. . . . It was me and my older sister and all I remember like right now is a plate dropping on the floor and all these finger wedges go on the floor. My sister, my older sister running to the stove, turning the stove off, calling my mom Bs and whores and fiends and crackheads, calling her all these different names. . . . But my mom started crying, and she still did the drug. So how could you cry and still do the drug? How could you use the drug as an excuse to get over your feelings? How could you use the drug as an excuse, period?

Jeremiah could not reconcile his mother's promises to stay clean with her actions. Seeing his mother repeatedly fail to take on a maternal role left him helpless and traumatized him.

In contrast to most other families in this study, his aunt and grandmother were aware of Jeremiah's situation and made an effort to address his emotional challenges. His aunt asked him to come to stay with her in Illinois. She lives in a suburb of Chicago with her husband and two children. Ms. Lewis remembers that Jeremiah did not handle the culture shock well. He didn't fit in, and his presence challenged her own position in the upper-class, predominantly white community. Shortly after his arrival Jeremiah started hanging out with the teenage sons of her neighbors. He began telling lies and tried to talk them into handing over their gadgets: "They had a lot of cool toys and he said, can I have that? That was not a good look for me. My nephew's here visiting and he's begging them for their stuff," she explains.

In the end Ms. Lewis sent Jeremiah home because he was disrespectful to her and her husband, slamming doors, not taking into consideration that there were young children in the house. Two weeks after she had put him on plane back to Philadelphia, he committed the crime that led his current four-to-eight-year sentence for aggravated assault. Jeremiah's case shows how difficult it is even for middle-class African American families to protect their children. Jeremiah's family was not poor but lived close to inner-city poverty. Different from white families in their situation, their child was vulnerable to the influences of the gangs that crossed over from the disadvantaged areas that were close by, and the schools that Jeremiah attended lacked the resources of affluent white areas (Pattillo-McCoy 1999). As part of one of the few black families in her affluent suburb, Jeremiah's aunt was aware that her nephew's actions might play into the stereotypes of their neighbors. She likely did not want to risk the social equilibrium she had achieved for her children. Jeremiah was better off than most of the young men I interviewed. His family's social capital nevertheless did not match the economic resources and social ties that a white middle-class family would have had facing a similar situation.

CONCLUSION

Parental drug and alcohol abuse are interwoven in the young men's recollections of their childhood in many different ways. While Dylan, Gabriel, and Jordan experienced extreme poverty, and physical as well as emotional abuse, Jeremiah mostly struggles with the emotional fallout of his mother's continuous absence and unreliability. All of them had to confront their parents' erratic behavior and repeated failure to provide for their basic needs. It is easy to comprehend why juvenile justice interventions failed to reach these young men. Their parents had disconnected from their caregiving roles and counted on their children to take care of themselves and their younger siblings. Especially Dylan, Jordan, and Gabriel were not used to any protective adult presence in their life. When they came of age, they overestimated their ability to live an adult life not just because that is what teenagers do, but also because they did not know how to function within the parameters others tried to impose on them.

Parental substance-abuse issues are one of several contingent social circumstances that co-occurred with violent criminal behavior. For a majority of African American respondents, their parents' drug addiction cemented the family's abject poverty. It exacerbated residential instability and other social ills of poverty. Even when, as in Jeremiah's case, the underlying poverty did not reach levels of desperation, witnessing a mother's emotional unraveling left irreparable emotional scars. Those emotional struggles made it difficult for Jeremiah to work through his challenges at school and to withstand the sense of belonging that gang membership seemed to offer.

Over the past decades qualitative sociological and criminological research almost exclusively focused on how government institutions criminalize especially minority men (Goffman 2014; Shedd 2015; Van Cleve 2016). In his seminal work *In Search for Respect* Bourgois (2002: 11f) warns that "countering traditional moralistic biases and middle-class hostility toward the poor should not come at the cost of sanitizing the suffering and destruction that exists on the inner-city streets." As scholars and public intellectuals focus on mass incarceration, labeling, overpolicing, deviance as resistance, or the school to prison pipeline (Cohen 2004; Alexander 2010; Rios 2011; Shedd 2015; Kupchik 2016), careful analysis of destructive behavioral responses to extreme disadvantage has been sidelined in the discipline and in public discourse. Describing how parental drug addiction relates to juvenile criminal behavior may still be a slippery slope and could easily be interpreted as victim-blaming.

Presenting the young men's narratives in their full complexity does not have to lead us to the conclusion that they are part of a dysfunctional "culture of poverty" and in dire need of middle-class role models (Wilson 1990; Lewis 1975). The narratives rather demonstrate that abject poverty is crippling. The young men's descent into criminal behavior is as much rooted in structural neglect as it is connected to individual parenting failures. A society that proclaims everyone's right to "the pursuit of happiness" has the duty to protect children from the extreme poverty that takes over when parents succumb to drug-seeking behaviors.

Parental drug addiction, in particular, shaped criminal trajectories directly and indirectly. Especially parents who were addicted to crack or opioids opened up opportunities for criminal behavior. They left children unsupervised for prolonged periods and allowed them to witness and eventually participate in drug dealing and consumption on a regular basis. Young men whose parents struggled with addiction also were at higher risk of experiencing trauma and deprivation. Parents neglected their children, who often came home to an empty fridge and lacked clothes that they could wear to school. They faced a reverse "maturity gap" and had to take on adult responsibilities when they were still children. Since they were used to taking care of themselves from an early age, it was likely difficult for them to accept directions from any adults, especially when it involved representatives of a rule-bound juvenile justice system.

When it comes to drug addiction, public policy tends to focus on the short-term effects of addiction. The potential long-term traumatic effect that a caregiver's addiction has on a child is understudied and remains politically unaddressed. While "crack babies" grabbed headlines at the height of the epidemic, there has been no concerted governmental effort to support the children of the crack epidemic into their adulthood.

From a generational perspective Dylan, Gabriel, Jordan, and Jeremiah are second-generation victims of the crack epidemic. They were not addicted to the drug, but they grew in a community that still had not fully healed from the destruction crack had wreaked at the familial and neighborhood levels (Contreras 2013). Focusing on this group is an important reminder that social problems as extreme as the crack epidemic cause persistent trauma across generations.

The narratives again demonstrate that abject poverty is crippling. Poor people are not allowed to make mistakes. When they do, it exacerbates their already tenuous existence. Even more so, when African American parents make wrong decisions, racism, concentrated poverty, and a powerful criminal justice apparatus make it even more difficult for them to overcome their marginal social position.

The wealthy, on the other hand, may consume drugs and they may neglect their children, but their actions do not have the same devastating consequences. Layers of privilege established over generations shield all but the most extreme cases from the consequences the poor have to bear almost immediately. Once we address self-destructive choices, like drug addiction, from within the framework of structural inequality, we may be able to develop a better understanding of how criminal behavior manifests over time and how we can more effectively support families who suffered through trauma and continue to live at the fringes of American society.

4. The Weakness of Strong Ties

Extreme Poverty and the Fracture of
Close Kinship Ties

On a September afternoon in 2010 Miguel got dressed in sweatpants, a gray sweater, and black Nike Airs. Probably, he put his black wig and the Pirates baseball cap on last, just before he left his friend's apartment. The friend with whom he had been staying drove him to a corner, just a few blocks away from the local M&T Bank. He was going to pick him up again when everything was done. Miguel walked into the bank and dropped a blue backpack at the front door. In his hand he held something that vaguely looked like a detonator. He told the bank tellers that the backpack contained a bomb. He would explode it if they didn't give him money.

There was no bomb in the backpack and the money he received had a GPS tracking device attached to it. Miguel was arrested almost as soon as he left the bank. His friend never came to pick him up. When the police stopped him, Miguel didn't run. At the precinct he told the officers who questioned him that he was homeless and unemployed. By the time Miguel decided to become a bank robber, his life had been a succession of parental abandonment, abuse, educational failure, and self-destructive choices. He felt that he had nothing to lose.

While Miguel's case is extreme, even within the group of the thirty young violent offenders I interviewed, the experience of ruptured kinship ties resurfaces repeatedly when the young men narrativize their lives. The breaking of what we usually consider strong ties between child and caregiver is a traumatic event in its own right. It symbolizes the ultimate destructive impact that poverty has on severely disadvantaged families and often comes on the heels of other trauma, such as food and housing insecurity or parental mental health problems. Growing up in extreme poverty can put unusual pressure on close kinship ties. Especially, when extreme resource deprivation meets the emotional volatility of adolescence, close ties between parents and their children can break. In a post-welfare era disadvantaged adolescents and their parents cannot fall back on a kinship network or social services that could substitute for broken parental ties (Miller-Cribbs and Farber 2008). Many of the young men in this study were left to fend for themselves, and being disconnected from their familial unit became a catalyst for their criminal behavior.

Social scientists have long tried to understand how social ties operate in poor communities. In *All Our Kin*, Carol Stack (1974) shows that kin networks in poor neighborhoods may defy middle-class standards but are far from dysfunctional. She argues that extended fictive kinship ties can take the place of the traditional nuclear family and offer the kind of support one would expect from close kin. Over the past decades scholars have relativized Stack's depiction of family life in poor neighborhoods (Brewster and Padavic 2002; Sarkisian and Gerstel 2004; Miller-Cribbs and Farber 2008; Levine 2013). Matt Desmond (2012), in particular, set the stage for understanding how poverty undermines the social fabric of disadvantaged communities. He argues the poor utilize "disposable ties" to cope with housing insecurity. Rather than relying on kin, they quickly form close connections to strangers. Those bonds, born out of necessity, are discarded once they cease to be useful.

Building on Desmond's observation, I argue that network volatility also reaches the core of poor families. Overwhelmed by financial responsibilities mothers and fathers engage in emotional and financial triage. The limited emotional and material resources they have tend to be expended on the youngest children living in the household (Lareau 2003). In fact, as I showed in chapter 3, several young men had to take care of themselves and their siblings when their parents were unable to fulfill a provider role.

While middle-class children remain financially connected to their parents at least until they finish college in their mid-twenties, the families I interviewed had often severed financial ties to their sons during the early years of adolescence. The pressure that extreme poverty places on families may break ties between parents and children prematurely. Without strong social connections to adults, the respondents' pathways into crime accelerated during their early teenage years until their adjudication in the adult criminal justice system.

SOCIAL TIES, POVERTY, AND CRIME

The family structure of poor African Americans has occupied sociologists and historians since the beginning of the twentieth century (Frazier 1939;

Moynihan 1965). Arguments about severed kinship ties inevitably evoke the specter of the "culture of poverty" argument (Lewis 1975). In the early 1990s William Julius Wilson developed a more nuanced, but still widely debated iteration of Lewis's concept. In *The Truly Disadvantaged* Wilson (1990) argues that desegregation allowed middle-class blacks to leave the inner city behind. Those who remained lacked role models; civic institutions disintegrated and single motherhood became the norm in such communities. Taking a historical perspective, Orlando Patterson (1998) argues that the prevalence of single motherhood in the African American community is a cultural practice that originated during slavery. Slave owners discouraged and even punished the formation of nuclear families.

In this long line of highly contested arguments about African American family structures, Carol Stack's aforementioned 1974 study *All Our Kin* represents a watershed moment. Her argument about reciprocal exchange within extended kin networks challenges the notion that African American families are dysfunctional because they don't replicate the nuclear family model. As Stack argues, extended kin networks are an effective way of distributing resources in an environment where economic opportunities are limited. *All Our Kin* has long influenced how sociologists discuss family dynamics in the inner city. Similar to Stack's observations Edin and Lein (1997) find that poor single mothers creatively rely on their social networks to balance their multiple needs. In their study of low-income women, Dominguez and Watkins (2003) discover similar dynamics. The women they interviewed utilize family members for social support.

Yet, even though some studies have at least partially supported Stack's argument, the empirical evidence in support of strong kin networks and high levels of trust in disadvantaged neighborhoods is dwindling (Sampson and Graif 2009; Roschelle 1997; Wacquant and Wilson 1989). Brewster and Padavic (2002), for instance, show that the number of African American mothers relying on kin for childcare significantly declined between 1977 and 1994. In their overview of the current state of research on kin networks among poor African Africans, Miller-Cribbs and Farber (2008) also conclude that the assumption of kinship networks as a reliable source of support is not valid anymore. Especially in homogenous networks composed of resource-poor members, a meaningful exchange of financial or material support is very challenging.

Miller-Cribbs and Farber's assessment resonates with Levine's work. In *Ain't No Trust* (2013), she observes that the welfare reform created a high degree of uncertainty in the lives of single mothers. This insecurity, she argues, corrodes the establishment of trusting lateral and hierarchical relationships. In a post-welfare society this kind of network instability affects poor white families as much as it does minorities. Sarkisian and Gerstel (2004) show that kin support varies according to class position rather than race. Socioeconomic status, they argue, drives the kind of kin support someone can provide. Since African Americans are on average poorer than whites, they may not be able to offer substantial monetary help to relatives in need. Qualitative data show that poor white single mothers operate under extensive constraints as well when tapping their social network for emotional and material support. Those mothers carefully manage even ties to close kin to avoid the impression of being in a unilateral exchange relationship (Nelson 2000; Blau 1986).

Desmond (2012) also observes that the poor may turn to others who share a similar life situation rather than seeking help from close kin securely anchored in the middle class. Since these relationships lack mutuality and are in most cases unilateral, better-off kin may become exasperated by repeated requests for help. Forming ties to strangers thus becomes a way of coping with housing insecurity. These ties become intense very fast and dissolve almost as quickly once they have fulfilled their function.

The world of readily available kin support may have vanished in the wake of welfare reform, though it is important to note that residents of poor neighborhoods are not simply "bowling alone" (Putnam 2000). While some ties are kept at a distance, other relationships can still be used as a source of material and emotional support. In coining the term "selective solidarity," Raudenbush (2016) strikes a middle ground. In the poor African American housing project she studies, the desire to shield oneself from others and their potential demands for support coexists alongside "meaningful exchange relationships" (1018).

The caregivers and youths I spoke to are at the extreme end of the poverty distribution. The young men had committed violent crimes when they were still children. Their families were plagued with food and housing insecurity, drug abuse, and illness. Without a doubt, the families in this study had difficulties maintaining reciprocal relationships. Even if we assume persistent, strong, extended kin networks in poor communities, those who cannot reciprocate services will inevitably be excluded (Stack 1974; Edin and Lein 1997; Desmond 2012). The data I present in this chapter therefore do not call into question the existence of supportive networks in poor communities. In fact, assuming "selective solidarity" allows me to focus on those very poor families who are not only left behind by the welfare reform but also likely excluded from any informal exchange networks persisting in low-income neighborhoods (Raudenbush 2016).

SOCIAL TIES AND CRIMINAL BEHAVIOR

With the advances of social network analysis criminologists are able to identify the kind of social ties that may or may not facilitate criminal behavior.[1] As previous research on the criminogenic effect of familial networks demonstrates, having a parent or sibling who is involved in crime increases the risk of becoming an offender (Row and Farrington 1997; Farrington et al. 2001; Bijleveld and Wijkman 2009; Beijers et al. 2017). Especially for young children, family networks are an important aspect of their socialization (Dewey 1988), and the relationship between growing up in a broken and abusive home and juvenile delinquency has been established strongly and repeatedly.

The seminal study *Unraveling Juvenile Delinquency* (Glueck and Glueck 1950) shows that teenagers who intersected with the criminal justice system tend to come from homes with parents who are either dead or divorced. A majority of the delinquent teenagers in the Gluecks' study also had violent substance abusers as caretakers. The level of family attachment across this group was significantly lower than that of well-adjusted children. In the mid-1980s, Rolf Loeber and Magda Stouthamer-Loeber (1986: 29) already concluded that "lack of parental supervision, parental rejection, and parent-child involvement, are among the most powerful predictors of juvenile conduct problems and delinquency."

Based on this previous work, I argue that the tenuous state of social ties between children and their caregivers significantly shaped the respondents' criminal trajectory. The lack of parental supervision and the absence of a functional social network generated opportunities for criminal behavior (Felson and Cohen 1979; Ary et al. 1999). The absence of caregivers also created the reverse maturity gap introduced in chapter 3. As I have shown, the young men had to take care of themselves and their younger siblings before they were physically, emotionally, and cognitively able to do so. Finally, the severance of strong social ties and its aftermath was in itself a traumatic event that impacted the respondents emotionally and cognitively (Terr 1991).

It is important to note that poverty already correlates with higher levels of opportunity for crime and traumatic events. The fracture of a strong tie between parents and children therefore increases the possibility that already-present environmental conditions pull and push teenagers further down the pathway toward crime (McLeod 2008).

The data show that there are multiple, overlapping ways that lead to the fracture of what we generally understand to be strong ties between caregivers and children. In most cases, it is impossible to pinpoint exactly which

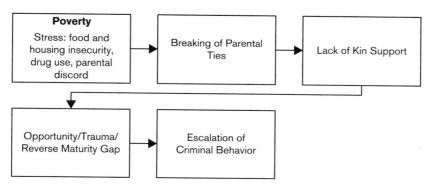

FIGURE 1: Escalation of Criminal Behavior
Source: Michaela Soyer, author

chain of events led to a disconnection between caregiver and children. Micro-social units break, for example, when mothers or fathers die untimely and unexpectedly. Death of a caregiver may be related to drug addiction, criminal involvement, or mental health issues. In very disadvantaged families, relatives who could assume parental roles are already overburdened. While they may take orphaned children in, they hardly have the emotional and material resources to care for them after a traumatic live-changing event.

Drug addiction contributes to the dissolution of familial ties, even if it does not lead up to death through an overdose. As has been elaborated in chapter 3, being addicted to alcohol or drugs incapacitates caregivers to such an extent that they disconnect even from small children. Two caregivers I interviewed dealt with unaddressed mental and physical health problems that not only added to the family's general economic insecurity, but also hastened the emotional disconnection between parents and children.

All of the families I met struggled with extreme economic hardship. Drug use, untreated physical and mental health problems, and eventually their children's criminal behavior further destabilized what was already a precarious struggle for survival. Despite each family's idiosyncratic web of misfortunes, the common pattern that emerges is clear: The group of young offenders I interviewed confronted the breaking of strong ties early in their lives. In all but one case, the extended kinship network was not able to compensate for the severance of those social connections. The cases described below represent the larger themes I was able to solicit from the data. Since the narratives reveal many interrelated struggles, I have grouped the data around the events or chronic problems that took center stage in the respondents' recollections. Figure 1 summarizes the chain of events that I observed in the data.

MENTAL HEALTH AND HOUSING INSECURITY

There is no direct line that leads from Miguel's childhood to him threatening to blow up a bank. However, his pathway into crime cannot be understood independently from his upbringing. Miguel says that he was eleven years old when he became homeless for the first time. He and his stepfather didn't get along. Miguel claims he tried to prevent his stepfather from hitting his mother and, as Miguel puts it, she "ended up choosing my stepfather over me." His mother threw him out of the house and after spending a few nights in the park, his older brother found him and allowed him to stay with him. From then on he started moving around among his multiple siblings, his biological father, and his aunt.

Miguel believes his mother was never there for him. She would just disappear for days without telling him where she was or when she was going to come back. When Miguel was a teenager his grandmother disclosed that her daughter—Miguel's mother—had been diagnosed with bipolar disorder. In the light of this diagnosis his mother's erratic behavior began to make sense to him. She "just blacked out and she started hitting me in the face with her wedding ring. Smashed me in the face and I was probably about thirteen, twelve when this was happening," he recalls. She went from throwing things at him to apologizing for not having taken her medication within moments.

The extended kin network Miguel relied on was far from supportive and stable and it could not compensate for his mother's mental illness. Everyone around him struggled to make ends meet. As a teenager he was unlikely to reciprocate any resources expended on him (Blau 1986). For his extended kinship network he was another mouth to feed. When things became tight financially with whomever he was staying at the moment, he was the first one who had to leave.

Like Miguel, Marc didn't have much when he grew up. He is very quiet and ashamed of the crimes he has committed. "I just wish I did make the right decisions back then," he says, and adds after a short pause, "I kind of, I still beat myself up about it. Not only did I harm those people; I mean I hurt my family as well." There is a sadness and vulnerability in his demeanor that makes it difficult to connect the young man in front of me to the crimes he committed when he was only fifteen. Back in 2009, he robbed five people during a single night. He is serving nine to twenty years for his crimes.

For a long time during Marc's childhood, his family did not manage to stabilize their housing. His mother was evicted so many times that he has trouble writing down all the addresses he lived at before he was incarcerated at fifteen. It is dizzying to follow his narrative of the families' many moves he can remember.

> I missed like a year of school, and that's when we got evicted from the projects and moved to Upper Darby. From Upper Darby, I was gonna go live with my grandfather . . . but ended up living with my grandmother. I started going to B. [another school], which is in West Philly. So my grandmother would drop me off at my grandfather's house, and I'd go to school from there. After my grandmother, we started living with my aunt and uncle. . . . Then, my grandmother, I think she got evicted from where she was staying at, so she moved to South Philly . . . . So, I lived with my grandmother and my uncles, which is her kids, my mother's brothers. Then from South Philly we moved to North Philly with my stepfather and his mom and his brother. Then, we moved from my stepfather's place up to some lady, I didn't really know her like that, but my mom moved in with some lady and her brother in West Philadelphia. . . . From there I moved to Houston, Texas. [Then] my mom got her own house. I moved back to Philadelphia. I came back from Houston, Texas, when I was twelve, I believe. I don't think I started school 'til I was fourteen.

From his account it is obvious that Marc's childhood, and more specifically his schooling, was interrupted by his family's inability to secure a stable place to live. The evictions took a psychological toll on him as well. Marc remembers, "There were like times where, I didn't wanna wake up. . . . I just wanted to go back to sleep. Just sleep forever." He has been struggling with depression for a long time, but has only been formally diagnosed since he arrived at Pine Grove.

Marc's mother and his sister recall that he was a regular child who was silly and liked to be around groups of people. According to his mother, Marc began getting into trouble when he was fourteen years old. Marc agrees that his behavioral problems started around that age. "I started leavin' the house, cursin' at my mom, and things like that," he says.

Even though his mother and sister insist that he used to be open and talkative, his mother remembers that he was diagnosed with post-traumatic stress disorder. He and his uncle were robbed at gunpoint. He had been seeing a therapist for about two months when he was arrested. His mother believes that the robbery put him over the edge. She recalls that he started hanging out with a group of boys who had a bad influence on him.

His mother was overwhelmed with parenting Marc. While he didn't want to stay in the house, do homework, or go to school, she was busy trying to keep a roof over the family's head. Getting Marc back into school, after he had returned from Houston, for example, became secondary. She tried to homeschool him but didn't have a computer and never managed to formally register him as homeschooled. Two years passed until Marc was reenrolled in the Philadelphia public school system.

Around the time Marc was arrested, his father's drug consumption also became an issue again. Marc's mother remembers that he used Marc as a go-between to extract money for drugs from his own father, Marc's grandfather. "It was just a whole lot, his dad was in and out of his life basically most of his life," she explains. The night Marc was arrested his mother wanted him to stay at home. She remembers fighting with him and trying to prevent him from leaving. Eventually she was fed was up with him and "put him out." A day later she felt guilty and started looking for Marc. The kids up the street told her that he had been arrested.

Marc hesitates when I ask him why he started committing crimes in the first place. He talks about how the poverty of his family ate away at him and he felt as if he had to do something about it. "I was young and thought it was the right thing to do. I felt good about it at the time. . . . I got the chance to actually bring some money to my mom even though it really wasn't much, but . . . at least I could help."

Marc's explanation can be read as shifting blame away from him. The stigma he felt growing up poor, however, is undeniable. It is also obvious that his mother was preoccupied with securing the bare minimum for the family while his father was struggling with addiction. When I asked her what she believes she could have done differently she replies: "I think I did the best that I could. As much as I could."

OVERWHELMED KIN

Unlike inner-city poverty, rural poverty in Pennsylvania is hidden amidst beautiful rolling hills. Shed-like dwellings, such as Andrew's home, are rendered nearly invisible among the picturesque red barns, towering grain silos, grazing cows, and the occasional Amish buggy. Andrew's grandparents are frail and struggling financially. When I visited them in the fall of 2014, they solely relied on the grandmother's Social Security checks for income. Andrew's grandmother used to work in a nursing home, but her back pain has made it impossible for her to do the physically taxing work of a nurse's aide.

Andrew, who is of mixed-race, refers to his grandparents as his real parents. "My mom and dad is Ann and Jim," he explains, "They're supposed to be my grandparents, but they're my mom and dad. They raised me. They fed me. They took care of me." He adds: "My mom . . ., when we benefit her, that's when she wants to be a mom." Andrew's grandparents also recall that their daughter was never interested in raising Andrew and his sister. "There was never a bond [between her and Andrew]; even when he was a tiny baby, she wouldn't get up and feed him in the middle of the night," the grandmother remembers. Andrew's case shows that even when relatives are willing and emotionally ready to fulfill a parental role, they may lack the financial resources and the social capital to raise an emotionally challenging child.

Ann is stooped and uses a cane to get around. The grandparents' house is small and dark, with an unfinished floor and worn furniture. Andrew's grandfather was one of thirteen children. He dropped out of school and began to work for his father, who owned a garbage truck. Jim didn't learn how to read and write until he joined the army in his early twenties. Jim's father, Andrew's great-grandfather, had violent outbursts. He used a rake to hit his son over the head. Jim emphasizes that he wants to parent differently than the violent, erratic man he knew growing up. Andrew's grandparents used their limited financial resources and enrolled him in sports. They recall that they tried to keep him busy after school, but when Andrew turned sixteen, he began stealing his grandparent's painkillers and selling them.

His grandfather believes that Andrew was doing fine until he fell in with the wrong crowd. "We couldn't talk to him. We go to bed; he'd climb out the window and go all night long. He came home early in the morning before we ever get up. He wouldn't go to school. He only had about three months of school left. He wouldn't go back," he remembers. Andrew's grandparents were overwhelmed with raising a teenager. They consciously decided to forego physical punishment, but they also did not know what type of parental discipline could take its place. Both of them blame their age for missing crucial signs that their grandson was in trouble. His grandparents tried as best as they could do to fill the void Andrew's mother had left. Yet, as Andrew spiraled out of control and their physical health declined, they were unable to effectively intervene.

Andrew's aunt, his other strong familial tie, further destabilized him even as she provided additional emotional support. Andrew believes that his aunt has particularly bad taste in men: "My aunt . . . pulls people into her problems 'cause she's an idiot. I don't know how someone so smart could be so freaking dumb." She also played a crucial role in introducing him to drug dealing. He recalls that his aunt's boyfriends were involved in drug dealing and burglaries. He insists: "I didn't get dragged or pushed into anything. I just saw what they were doing, and I'm like, oh I wanna do that."

Andrew is comparatively lucky. He has grandparents who love him and care for him. They continued to be on his side even when he was arrested again shortly after his release from Pine Grove in the fall of 2014. Andrew's ties to his grandparents are not emotionally tenuous but rather structurally fragile. Because of their age and health problems, it is unclear how long they will be able to support their grandson. Likewise, while his aunt was emotionally there for him, she also exposed him to the influence of older men who were already involved in crime (Harding 2010).

Luke is the oldest in a family of six children. His father was addicted to drugs and died of a heroin overdose in 2005, when Luke was only eleven years old. His mother had separated from Luke's father soon after her son was born. She took her son to live with her family in Erie but returned to Philadelphia after two years. There she remarried and had five more children. Her youngest child, another son, died of SIDS when he was eight months old in 2006.

Luke's relationship with his stepfather was strained: "Him and my ex, the father of my daughters, they didn't get along," his mother remembers. Luke admits that he stole his stepfather's money, but he also remembers his stepfather coming home drunk regularly. "He's fighting with my mom, and he starts yelling at her . . . [When] he comes home drunk I . . . feel on edge. I don't know what's gonna happen next. . . . It makes me mad, makes me snap out."

When the tension between Luke and his stepfather escalated, it was Luke who had to leave. He was used to getting kicked out and "then just staying with whoever I could stay with at the time." When his stepfather refused to let Luke come home definitively, his mother sent him to live with his biological father. Luke loved his father: "When he wasn't getting high, he was a real good person," he says. Those moments were rare, however: "He was . . . home for a little bit, not getting high, then he'll start getting high or he'll be in jail." Even when his father was sober he was still in the streets and Luke understood what was going on: "I knew things at certain ages that I shouldn't, shouldn't have known." Luke's father was an ineffective parent at best and negatively influenced his son at worst. His father was the first one to introduce Luke to smoking marijuana. Luke recalls that he was seven years old when his father started offering weed to him: "It'd be like once a month, it was like maybe a joke. Like he would get like a kick out of it, I guess it was funny to him," Luke speculates.

When Luke's mother realized that his father's drug consumption had gotten out of control, she managed to take him back home. Luke didn't stay there for very long though. When he was fifteen, he moved in with his uncle, who himself was struggling with addiction. This living arrangement lasted about six months. His uncle told him to leave when Luke stopped attending school regularly. At sixteen Luke was living alone. He supported himself robbing other drug dealers. Luke remembers this time almost fondly: "I could do whatever I wanted whenever I wanted to, I didn't have to listen to nobody. I didn't have no rules." When he was seventeen he was arrested for armed robbery. After being out on bail for thirteen months he was sentenced to three to ten years for robbery. When I interviewed Luke he had been at Pine Grove for two years. His mother had not been there to visit him.

When I speak to her about her relationship to her son, her emotions sway back and forth between feeling remorse about her parental failures and being disappointed in Luke. She regrets most that she did not pay attention to him and his emotions: "When he needed me most," she explains, "I was raising four babies. All my girls are a year apart." While she feels like "a bad mom" she also does not know what she could have done different. Luke's mother believes that "life took a toll" on them. Her eight-month-old son's sudden death taxed her already difficult relationship with her second husband and destabilized the family. Like most of the young men I interviewed, Luke did not have a social network that could have supported him when his mother was stricken with grief and preoccupied with raising her younger children.

DEATH OF A CAREGIVER

Tyler, a twenty-two-year-old African American from Harrisburg, received a five-to-twelve-year sentence for robbery. When I interviewed him, he had been incarcerated for four years. None of his family had visited him so far. Tyler says that he doesn't want anybody to come and see him. He remembers visiting his father and uncles in prison and recalls that he hated the fact that they couldn't come home with him after visitation time was over.

Tyler explains that he would not want to re-create this feeling for anybody visiting him. He barely speaks to his family on the phone either: "I don't like to call home because every time I call home it's like something happened. . . . Either like somebody got shot or somebody shot somebody and they're getting sentenced. I don't have time for that . . . because I'm in a position where I can't do nothin'." The turmoil that surrounds his social network on the outside has been a constant aspect of his life: "Every male figure in my life has been locked up, down to my grandfather and great-grandfather." His expectations for his future had always been low: "You either get locked up, or get shot, or you shoot somebody."

Attributing Tyler's trajectory to a lack of male role models, however, does not capture the complexity of his childhood. His formative moment goes back more than eighteen years, when he witnessed his mother's death. When I asked him about the last memory he has of his mother he responded with a vivid recollection of her last moments:

> I wanted to go outside, I remember. She was like, no, we just gonna sit here and watch TV. She made me something to eat, and we sat on the couch. She sat on the couch right beside me. I still remember I was watching *Power Rangers*. I mean, so I'm like Mom, you see that, you see that? And she's talking to me, I mean, and her head was just tilted back. The couch, she wasn't sitting on the couch, you could rest your head. I remember her head was tilted back. I'm looking up like she fell asleep, so I watched cartoons for like another couple of seconds. Then, I'm like Mom, Mom, wake up. And I remember I'm pushing her, and she just slid over, so I looked, I'm like, I'm trying to wake her up. I'm like, Mom, Mom, wake up. She's not waking up, so that's when I ran to the bathroom to grab these pills I always seen her take. I grabbed a glass of water, and I put the pills in her mouth and poured the water in her mouth to try to get her to swallow. I just remember like the pill just floating in her mouth, so I knew something was wrong. That's when I started yelling and screaming and stuff.

He was alone in the home and his memories are fuzzy when it comes to recalling how exactly he tried to get help. Tyler scored a seventy-seven on the Wechsler Adult Intelligence Scale–Revised, which puts him in the category of being borderline mentally impaired. He only learned to read after he was admitted to state prison. While his low IQ may be indicative of his limited schooling rather than actual mental capacity, he struggles to make sense of the traumatic event that shaped his childhood. He doesn't know his mother's cause of death, for example. He claims, however, to have received a settlement for malpractice.

Witnessing his mother's death severely destabilized his psychological well-being. Tyler remembers that he used to be fascinated with fires even before his mother died. Setting fires became a way to cope with his traumatic memories: "I'd find plastic stuff and set it on fire and just watch it burn. . . . The colors made me forget. It gave me like a rush like you know like, wow. Just you could be so close to something that could kill you so fast. But just, I didn't know that at the time. But, it just gave me a rush because it made me forget, that's the reason I light it, it made me forget."

When he entered elementary school Tyler was quickly identified as a problematic child. He got into fights easily. As he remembers he just wanted to spend his breaks alone: "I didn't swing on the swings, all I wanted to do was just sit on a tree and be by myself. So, I guess like I'm not normal. 'Cause I don't wanna play. I just don't feel like damn playing." Tyler resisted interventions of social workers and therapists. When I asked him why he did not like opening up about his mother's death, he replied: "To be truthful with you, I think they were just too damn nosey. They wanna be fascinated with somebody else's life 'cause they're not satisfied with their own."

Tyler's neighborhood in Harrisburg is a textbook example of twenty-first-century urban poverty. Rundown, early-century row houses line the streets where he grew up. The buildings are remnants of a time when home ownership was a reasonable goal, even for those at the lower end of the socioeconomic spectrum. What must have once been a lively area, filled with tenants striving for upward mobility, is now a deserted alley. Windows are nailed shut and trash is strewn across weed-clogged sidewalks. Tyler used to live in a mid-rise brick apartment building at the very end of the street. I rang several doorbells in an attempt to see if anyone would remember Tyler and his grandmother; nobody answered. I was never able get ahold of any of the contacts Tyler provided. However, after visiting the neighborhood he grew up in, it is reasonable to infer that his grandmother was very poor. Becoming the main caregiver for Tyler likely put tremendous financial strain on her. The financial struggles may have made it very difficult to engage with a severely traumatized child.

When I ask Tyler whether or not he believes that his grandmother loved him, he responds with uncertainty: "She said she loved me, I guess I gotta take her word for it. [But] I don't trust nobody." Tyler speculates that his grandmother probably felt an obligation to keep him out of the foster system. Tyler tried to make up for his dysfunctional family ties by connecting to people heavily involved in street crime. "I had people, that I thought that loved me and that were there for me," he remembers. People that wouldn't snitch and would have his back when things got violent and others were shooting at him.

Tyler's narrative demonstrates the discrepancy between the formal structure and the actual strength of his kin network. On the surface, his example fits traditional assumptions about an extended kin network willing to step in when ties break down (Stack 1974). Tyler's grandmother indeed took responsibility for raising her grandson. Tyler's memories of his childhood, however, indicate that his extended kin network was fragile and unable to help him cope with the loss of his mother.

CONCLUSION

In *All Our Kin* Carol Stack describes how inner-city African American families creatively redefine kinship. An expansive network of people helped each other to navigate life in a segregated neighborhood. Stack's work provided the necessary basis for a nuanced approach to unconventional family structures. It is important to keep in mind, however, that Stack collected her data when the United States still offered a viable social safety net. Stack respondents undoubtedly lived stressful and impoverished lives. Yet after the dismantling of the welfare system, poverty has become an even more devastating experience for families (Edin and Shaefer 2015).

In the spring of 2014, when I interviewed the young men in prison, I had just given birth to my second child. While I enjoyed getting out of the house and back into my work, I also struggled being away from my four-month-old for sometimes twelve hours at a stretch. Listening to the young men talking about how their mothers had abandoned them, how those who were supposed to take care of them did not provide a minimum of stability and security, was infuriating. This sentiment stayed with me until I visited their families and friends. I understood that mothers had not simply acted selfishly but rather had to deal with the constant stress and insecurity engulfing families making due with minimal resources (Edin and Shaefer 2015; Desmond 2016).

A reasonable functioning social welfare system like the Aid to Families with Dependent Children (AFDC) may have enabled extended kin networks to step in when the main provider of a child was either temporarily or even indefinitely incapacitated. The network of people surrounding the young men I interviewed struggled with addiction, housing instability, mental illness, unemployment, and criminal justice involvement. Nobody intervened effectively when Tyler, Luke, Andrew, or Trevor began committing crimes. On the contrary, families who were already preoccupied with making ends meet, managing younger siblings, and keeping their own drug addiction at bay may be more likely to disconnect from a family member who threatens the tenuous equilibrium. Fractured kinship ties and poverty shaped the teenagers social, cultural, and economic reality as they came of age. Based on what we know about the impacts that an unstable family, childhood trauma, and ultimately the lack of supervision have on juvenile delinquency, it is more than plausible that the disconnection of parental ties without a social network to extend financial and emotional support further accelerated the young men's criminal behavior.

5. Masculinity and Violence

Physical and Emotional Abuse at Home and in the Juvenile Justice System

The PADOC case summary files specify whether or not inmates have been victims of domestic abuse. Based on those files, only one of the young men was victimized as a child. During our interviews a very different picture emerged. Twelve respondents recall either witnessing or experiencing incidents of physical abuse during their childhood. Child abuse and neglect is significantly underreported in the general population as well (Dellafemina, Yeager, and Lewis 1990; Wood et al. 2016). It is difficult to imagine a social environment less conducive to openly talking about childhood victimization than a jail or prison. Counselors and other staff members struggle to create the kind of trust that would encourage inmates to share the trauma they have lived through (Soyer 2016). The discrepancy between official statements and the narratives I was able to solicit signify a deep distrust of government agencies. The underreporting of physical abuse, in particular, is also attributable to a specific understanding of masculinity. Many respondents frame their painful memories as adequate punishment for their transgressions and an important preparation for manhood.

In the first part of this chapter I focus on the young men's mistrust of government agencies, especially Pennsylvania's child protective agency. The respondents' suspicion of government intervention in combination with a specific understanding of masculinity ensured that they rarely disclosed any abuse to outsiders. Secondly, I show that the juvenile justice system, specifically the correctional personnel at the Glen Mills reform schools, perpetuated the same kind of distorted understanding of manhood, preventing the young men from speaking up about excessive use of force.

The young men's concept of masculinity made them more vulnerable and encouraged them to endure traumatizing verbal and physical abuse at home, on the streets, and in the juvenile justice system. Most respondents share a basic idea of what it means to act like a man. Enduring physical and emotional pain without complaining, for example, is considered a quintessential male attribute. For them, being a man not only means using violence on others but also accepting being victimized by others. Believing that "what doesn't kill you makes you stronger" also enabled them to navigate the different juvenile and criminal justice settings they passed through. In the end, this hypermasculine identity not only minimizes their own culpability, but diminishes their awareness that they have been victimized across multiple social settings.

BECOMING A MAGNIFICENT POKÉMON

When I interviewed Julian, he was serving four to seventeen years for aggravated assault. His mother and stepfather remember that Julian would always get into trouble for fighting. He was involved in drug dealing, but it was his violence that brought him to the Young Adult Offender program. Three years later he still vividly remembers the fateful confrontation that let to his adult conviction:

> It was the night before Halloween in 2010. It was me, her (his girlfriend), couple other girls, my man Jacobi. We were all drinking, having fun. And this dude walked past, and he gave the girl attitude that I was with. He was calling her all types of names and stuff. . . . So, I'm just standing there watching. She was like my boyfriend is gonna beat you up. . . . He's like I'll beat him the fuck up. . . . He called me all types of names. So, I punched him. And then like he came back at me, and I hit him again. Then, his nose broke or something. Something happened with his face, and it was over. . . . His face was bleeding. I gave him my shirt so he could wipe his face off. I told him to respect her, and he kept it moving. But he knew the girl that we were with, so when he went home he looked her up. And then, he found me through her on Facebook. And his dad filed charges. And I was already on state parole or state probation for another case I caught right before that.

Using physical violence as an expression of male dominance provides the backdrop for brutalizing others (Contreras 2013; Bourgois 2002). From Julian's perspective, this fight was purely about defending his girlfriend's honor. He ended it once his opponent stopped hitting back. Julian even made a final gesture of reconciliation: handing over his shirt so that his victim could wipe his bloody nose.

Julian's case summary file presents a more drastic version of the injuries he caused: The fifteen-year-old victim had a broken nose and a "large piece of flesh" was torn from his upper lip. He suffered from swelling to his head and face. The teenager had to have stents put into his nasal cavity, to be able to breath again through his nose.

Juxtaposing this version with Julian's sanitized recollection of the events clarifies the parameters of his male identity. Julian presents himself as responding to insults and repeated provocations. The way he describes his aggression, it is not deployed randomly but a reaction to disrespectful behavior and it is rule bound. For example, he emphasizes that he did not use needless violence after his competitor has given up. The scene he describes is more reminiscent of a boxing match than a random violent attack. Julian also wants to be perceived as someone who defends the weak. He says that he helped kids who were bullied in school. As his mother tells it, when people were not strong enough to fight for themselves, Julian would do it for them. "He wanted to save everybody," she explains.

As Julian reflects more on his motivations it becomes obvious that his "Robin Hood" narrative is too simplistic to describe his violent outbursts. He remembers that he started beating others up because it made for a good anecdote. Fighting, he recalls, was the cool thing to do. As he puts it: "Get into a good fight, then sit here and tell a story about how I fought the person. Everybody be laughing." His fights, however, had a darker side. Sometimes, he admits, "the anger came out of nowhere . . ., like blackouts and stuff." In the end, Julian admits, his fighting was not about helping others anymore. He remembers that he "was going out looking for people to mess up. . . . And then, like I would jump at the opportunity." Framing his actions as an assertion of masculine power utilized for protecting the weak, however, normalized his outbursts and prevented those around him from addressing the underlying pathology of his actions.

Josiah, a twenty-year-old black inmate from Pittsburgh, also evokes traditional male role behavior to justify his involvement in crime. When I interviewed him Josiah was serving a three-to-six-year sentence for robbery. Before entering the Young Adult Offender program he was mostly involved in drug dealing. As the only male in his family, he believed it was responsibility to take on a provider role. For a brief period, Josiah was legally employed. His job only paid $7.50 an hour, far less than what he could make dealing drugs. The massive "pay cut" he took working an entry-level food service job diminished his self-worth and undermined his patriarchal concept of supporting the women in his life. As Josiah puts it: "I'm surrounded by females, so females they got certain wants that they have. As far as like hair, nails, stuff like that. I'm making sure all that get done for them. And now, I can't even do it. I just felt, I didn't feel too good about myself. Yeah, I got a job and I'm making money but I'm still not able to provide." He also simply enjoyed having money to spend and getting admired for his success. The young boys in the neighborhood looked up to him and made him feel powerful and respected.

Especially respondents who grew up in areas of concentrated disadvantage tend to frame selling drugs as a way to take care of their families. Jesus explains that everyone around him was struggling to get by. The drug dealers he knows "need to sell their drugs, . . . they need to do that to survive, to stay afloat." Struggling with extreme deprivation, he says, "hardens your heart." When the opportunity to make money arises, Jesus argues, you take it without thinking about the consequences. In fact, getting arrested is not the worst thing that can happen to you. As Jesus explains: "The risk definitely outweigh the consequences . . . 'cause you can actually sit back when you sitting in a cell or a placement, like it was worth it. I fed my family. Or now my family be cool until I go home, it was worth it." Jesus recalls that he had already decided committing crimes was worth the risk when he was nine years old. "My ambition was only for one thing, to make it in the criminal world," he remembers. Jesus describes in binary terms the world in which he grew up. You can either be an addict or a dealer. He wanted to be "a winner," and not the "fiend that's out there committing sexual acts for a bag of heroin or a bag of crack." The drug dealers he saw on his way to school shaped his expectations about the kind of life he wanted to live. Jesus aspired to be "that drug dealer, being that guy driving around in a nice car, nice clothes, beautiful women."

Tyler remembers having a similar outlook life when he was involved in street life:

> You look at life like a Pokémon. You're a cute little mosh and now you gotta evolve like into this magnificent Pokémon. You feel me? So now, for you to do that, for people to see you as that magnificent Pokémon, you gotta do things to make them notice you. You doing things to make girls notice you, and you doing things to make the old heads get you respect now. You trying to show you got something, like you got a reason to be out here. So basically like you gotta, how we say it in the hood, either roll with it or get rolled on. You know?

For Jesus and Tyler it is important to come out on top, to take advantage of others rather than being taken advantage of. They displayed their success through fast-paced conspicuous consumption (Contreras 2013). Tyler recalls that he wanted to be like his uncle, who drove an expensive Mercedes SUV and had women so beautiful they looked to him as if they were not from this world.

Tyler did not learn how to read until he was sent to juvenile placement. Jesus, however, had educational opportunities opening up for him. He finished high school while he was in juvenile placement. When he took the SAT there, he received a score high enough to be admitted to Temple University. Although the juvenile justice system paid for his education he continued to be drawn to the streets. Jesus lost his funding when he violated the conditions of his probation. In the end, the prospect of getting a better-paying job after four years of college was too abstract in comparison to the quick money he could make selling drugs. Despite his high IQ of 115, he was not able to adapt his habitus to the scripts of middle-class institutions (Lareau 2003; Bourdieu 2001; Bourgois 2002; Cohen 1956).

MASCULINITY AND VICTIMIZATION

The "doing gender" paradigm asserts that gender is a malleable concept subject to negotiation and established in relation to the social environment (West and Zimmerman 1987). Messerschmidt (1993), who was among the first to introduce the idea of "doing gender" into criminology, argues that the disproportionate involvement of men in crime is related to masculinity enacted outside of institutional structures. Crime is a form of expressing masculinity when other resources for asserting male identity are absent.

In *Learning to Labor* Willis (1981) shows that working-class boys utilize a specific kind of masculinity to express their opposition to the middle-class culture that excludes them. The narratives of Julian, Josiah, Jesus, and Tyler are classic representations of this relationship between masculine habitus and criminal behavior. Julian expresses his masculinity through physical dominance over others. Josiah presents himself as the male provider who supports the lifestyle of the "females" in his family. Jesus and Tyler more explicitly than the other two admit that they were pursuing materialistic goals. All four practice what Adam Reich (2010) refers to as "outsider masculinity." Reich shows that men who embody outsider masculinity "conceptualize power, as something physical, worn on their bodies" (24). "Outsider masculinity" as a response to social closure thus becomes a trap that further alienates already marginalized young men from the middle class (ibid.).

The narratives also reveal that the young men fashioned their masculine habitus as a coping mechanism, a protective layer against a social environment that repeatedly brutalized them. Just as masculinity can be expressed differently depending on the individual's resources and social context, masculinity fulfilled different functions depending on the social situation in which the young men found themselves. The respondents also activated their masculine identity to cope with their own victimization. The script of masculinity, as something that is expressed physically, by leaving marks on someone's body, minimized their own physical and emotional pain. As much as this specific enactment of masculinity enabled the respondents to victimize others, it also made it easier for family members and outsiders to inflict pain on them.

KEEPING IT ALL IN THE FAMILY

Acting like a man means to assert power. "A real man," however, also has to accept when others inflict emotional and physical pain on him. The large majority of respondents who experienced emotional and physical abuse or neglect had not talked about it to anyone. Most of the young men who were maltreated at home or in the juvenile justice system did not even want to classify their experiences as a form of abuse or neglect.

When I ask Julian about his childhood he emphasizes that he was happy growing up. While Julian recalls many joyful memories, his home life was also volatile. Julian's biological father was in and out of prison during the ten years his parents stayed together. Julian's mother was fifteen when she was pregnant with her first child. Julian, her third one, was born right before his father went to prison for fifteen years for vehicular homicide. She met her second husband when Julian was two years old and had three more sons with him. Julian believes his mother and stepfather were emotionally overwhelmed and overworked. During our last interview he shared some memories of his mother's addiction to diet pills and his stepfather's crack habit. "It [the diet pills] would get her going, she's be up three or four days in a row," he remembers. He explains further, "She was zooming, she was like a cokehead." His stepfather would take crack intermittently but, as Julian says, he always made sure that he went to work and the bills were paid—he was "a functioning addict."

His mother and stepfather were fighting regularly in front of their children and Julian remembers them calling each other "crackhead" or "speed freak" during fights. Both of them would disappear overnight. His mother sometimes did not come back for several days in order to teach her husband a lesson about how hard it would be to run the family without her. Julian and his siblings also knew that his stepfather cheated on their mother. When he was old enough Julian tried to protect his younger siblings from the emotional chaos that engulfed his parents when they were fighting.

> I got to the point where I would just grab my little brothers and just go in the basement and play Playstation or something like that. I would take them away from it, so they didn't have to hear it. 'Cause me growing up, I sat there and I listened to it, I watched it. It's not

something that's fun. . . . It becomes normal, but that doesn't mean it doesn't hurt, you know?

Even though his parents' behavior was painful, Julian knew better than to share anything that happened at home with his teachers. He explains:

That was the major thing growing up. Like what happens in our house stays in our house. We don't tell. You don't tattletale. I grew up, don't tattletale, don't tattletale, don't tattletale. Don't talk. Don't speak to anyone that's officials. Don't talk to the teachers. Don't tell the teachers what's going on. That turned into: don't be a rat. Don't talk to the cops. Don't speak to these counselors.

The Philadelphia Department of Human Services did become involved when Julian's oldest brother told teachers that his mother and stepfather were beating him and that there were always parties at the house. Julian remembers that his brother "went to school and told them that he was being abused 'cause he didn't wanna live with us no more."

Most inmates I interviewed did not share anything about their family life with outsiders. They wanted to stay with their family, even if the living conditions were difficult. Jordan, for example, lied about his father's violent beatings rather than going into foster care. When a caseworker showed up at his father's house and asked Jordan about the bruises he had all over his body, he claimed he hurt himself playing football.

Jordan accepted abuse and neglect as part of his life. He remembers living in a dilapidated house in Chester around the time he started elementary school. His mother let everybody come in and hang out, as long as they put money in an envelope that was taped to the mailbox. People came there to hide guns and smoke crack. Back then, his father and grandmother were smoking crack as well. He remembers that he went to school with dirty clothes. Sometimes he stayed at home because he was too embarrassed about not having anything clean to wear. Once, he tried to wash his clothes in the sink and ended up going to school with his clothes all wet. While he realizes that his childhood lacked emotional and material stability he believes that it didn't hurt him, but made him more resilient: "I got locked up and stuff like that, but all around, I like the person I am right now," he says.

Tyler also suffered emotional and physical abuse during his childhood. He remembers: "When I was younger, like I used to get beat for no reason, used to get beatin's for stuff that other people did. It was easier just to blame it on me." When his grandmother abused him physically and emotionally after his mother's death, he also did not "cry" about it to anyone. It would never cross his mind to talk about his childhood to any of his peers, let alone to open up to somebody connected to the juvenile or criminal justice system.[1] Doing so would make him look weak. Tyler learned early on when he visited his father in prison that you "don't do something and cry about it at home later on." He believes men should simply deal with their problems alone rather than complaining to others about how difficult their life is:

> I'm not the type of person that's gonna cry. I'm not the type of person that just flips out and does all this wild ass shit. That's not me. . . . I think the only people who should be sensitive is females. So like I'm not the type of guy to listen to another man's problems. Like all right, you have problems, that's you. Like I don't wanna be a part of your problems. I don't wanna hear your problems. I'll listen to a female, 'cause that's a female, that's the role that you're supposed to play. You're supposed to listen to females, you know? But I'm not gonna sit there and listen to another grown-ass man complain about how his life is just fucked up. I don't care. Like it just doesn't, it doesn't make sense. Like you're a man, that's the role that you're supposed to take. If you don't like it then I don't know. It's too bad for you.

MISTRUST OF GOVERNMENT AGENCIES

The young men and their families did not turn to government agencies for support. Their mistrust went beyond the strained relationship between residents and the police (Fontaine et al. 2017). In fact, they tried to avoid disclosing any information with anyone who could potentially report their family to the Department of Health Services. After the dismantling of the welfare state, there was indeed very little beyond food stamps they could expect to receive from the government. The young men knew not to share information about their family life with outsiders. Telling a teacher, for example, about being beaten, might bring a Department of Health Services caseworker to their door, which could mean ending up in foster care.

As the respondents grew older their interactions with the government representatives were mostly limited to the juvenile justice system. While juvenile justice fulfilled caretaking functions, it did so from within a punitive framework (Soyer 2016). Given the interactions the young men and their families had with anyone "working for the government," it is not a surprise that they never reported the abuse they lived through to the social workers or clinicians they encountered in the juvenile or criminal justice system. The mistrust of government institutions, combined with the young men's skewed perception of physical violence, all but guaranteed that their physical and emotional abuse remained unreported.

TAKING A BEATING: ABUSE IN THE
JUVENILE JUSTICE SYSTEM

The young men's high tolerance for violence also played into the hands of the Pennsylvania juvenile justice system. Six of the thirty participants were held at Glen Mills, a renowned juvenile justice facility an hour outside of Philadelphia. All of them either witnessed or experienced firsthand that staff resorted to brutal beatings. While one of the respondents admits he could not handle the staff's violence and desired to leave, the others put up with it. Physical violence and emotional abuse were a normal part of their life. They also enjoyed the state-of-the-art exercise facilities and educational opportunities the facility had to offer.

Abuse allegations about Glen Mills' staff have surfaced repeatedly over the last decade. Newspaper articles and blog posts, easily recovered on the internet, testify to the extreme measures some staff members resort to when they want to enforce discipline at the school.[2] While anonymous posts on the internet are hardly a credible source, the range of material accessible online indicates that the Glen Mills Schools have a troubled history. The Connecticut Department of Children and Families, for example, stopped sending juveniles to the facility in 2012 because of the repeated abuse allegations.[3] The most recent piece, published in 2012, discusses a lawsuit brought by a former teacher who was fired when he reported that his supervisor hit a student in the face (Rose 2012). The more rampant form of abuse allegations seems to have taken place during to the late 2000s and early 2010s, around the time that the youth in my study would have been held at the facility.

The school's campus covers eight hundred acres and looks more like the grounds of an elite college than a juvenile justice placement center. A video yearbook, produced by the class of 2015–16, presents the facility as an institution that has helped young people to "better their lives" for 189 years. Red-brick buildings lead to the obligatory clock tower that oversees a meticulously maintained yard. The video shows young men harvesting pumpkins, eagerly immersed in books, and proudly walking to their graduation ceremony. The aerial shots at the beginning of the video also focus on the expansive sporting facilities: a track and field oval, a 750,000 square-foot recreation center. The young men in the 2015–16 video are playing football, basketball, and tennis. They are being trained in track, the shotput, and weightlifting.[4]

Glen Mills Schools are also well known internationally. During the mid-2000s German social scientists looked to Pennsylvania for different ways of engaging with delinquent youths and even began sending German youths there who were supposed to receive exceptional treatment and educational opportunities. Forty youths from Germany were being held at Glen Mills in 2005 and the school and the German press covered the school and its tactics widely.[5]

The cornerstone of the Glen Mills philosophy is a confrontational form of pedagogy. The school has established a buddy system in which each student is assigned a "buddy" to accompany him as he moves between different parts of the campus. The youths are supposed to hold each other accountable.[6] While the young men I interviewed were at Glen Mills, staff protocol adhered to the "seven levels of confrontation." Level seven, the final form of confrontation, allows staff to physically restrain youths (Foerstner and Weidner 2005). In 1989 Grant and Dubnov presented the Glen Mills model as a pathbreaking concept for modernizing failing reform schools in the United States. At that time supporters of Cosimo D. Ferrainola, executive director of the school between 1975 and 2007, praised his work effusively. The New York Times, for example, expressed unequivocal admiration for Ferrainola's leadership, asserting that "Glen Mills has evolved a culture that encourages self-discipline and a sense of mutual respect and responsibility."[7] What the six youths experienced in the late 2000s was a far cry from fostering "mutual respect." Staff members' excessive violence had festered in a pervasive culture of fear, displays of exaggerated masculinity, and silence.

Connor, a mixed-raced young man from the northern part of Pennsylvania, spent time in Glen Mills during his final placement just before he was adjudicated as an adult for robbery. When I ask him about his time in Glen Mills, he replies, "It's real nice, it's a big campus, it's got all the sports you can do." Especially, he adds, "if you stay on your path and you trying do something, [there are] a lot of good things you can do in Glen Mills." If you don't comply with the rules, on the other hand, staff can get physical. "Here [in Pine Grove]," Connor explains, "it's like getting sent to the hole or just getting a misconduct." In Glen Mills, "they take you in the back and they say they beat you up."

When I asked him what he means, he elaborates: "Well, it depends on what you did. Like, if you were fighting or you tried to run away, they punch you in your ribs, your face, your body, all over." Connor also remembers staff taking students into a back room and closing the door. He was called behind that door four times. Connor didn't mind the beatings as much though. He says that he knew what he was getting into when he went up there. Connor had heard already rumors about staff beating up students at Glen Mills before he arrived there. From his perspective physical violence was something he knew how to deal with. Also, Connor explains, "As long as you listened and did what you were supposed to do, you stayed out of trouble."

I pressed Connor to explain to me how it is possible that juvenile justice staff members get away with such blatant abuse. According to Connor there are several reasons that prevent the victims from speaking up. First, he explains, the phone booths that students use to call home are placed in earshot of the staff members. It was impossible to have confidential conversations. Secondly, Connor says that many parents believe their sons need this kind of discipline. They were in favor of the "ass whipping." Most young men, Connor believes, also don't say anything because they don't want to look weak. The attitude among students is: "'Don't complain like no little girl, you're supposed to be a grown man.' ... You go back there behind those doors [and] when you come out everybody been telling you 'alright, I got my ass whipped, I'm going to be a grown man about it.'"

Some of the violence that Connor witnessed during his almost two years there was even too much for him to stomach. He recalls a scene during lunchtime, when staff and students eat together: "The guy [a staff member] had a ring on. He was real big and he punched the kid in the eye and he split his eye [open]. The next day when I seen it and he had stitches and all that." Knowing that they had gone too far, Connor observed that the staff started being very nice to this student. He received new shoes and a new jacket. They let some of his transgression slide. "When they do your face real dirty like that, they start being nice to you," he explains. Once students gain privileges there is no incentive for them to speak up. Especially, as Connor points out, if they are in the program for several years, like he was. After all Connor had seen at Glen Mills, he still has fond memories of the school:

> I was up there [at Glen Mills] for two years, so naturally I got a lot of good memories, my track events, every time I participate in track. When I tried out for track and cross-country, going to the movies, lots of stuff.

Connor enjoyed Glen Mills so much that he did not want to go home. When I ask him what specifically he liked he replies: "Just everything, playing football up there. Cookouts up there. Going off campus up there. Going to the mall, walk around the mall. Playing games, playing video games."

I was very skeptical when the first respondent talked about the abuse he experienced at Glen Mills. My first assumption was the young man embellished his account to emphasize his victim role during the interview. After several respondents recalled similar incidents of violent staff behavior, it became evident that the abuse at Glen Mills was a recurring pattern. Connor's account in particular demonstrates how difficult it is for the students to even perceive their treatment as problematic. Connor discovered his aptitude for running the 800 meters at Glen Mills. For the first time, he felt valued and appreciate for his athleticism:

> In Glen Mills when I was running I got real real good at the sport I didn't know I was that good at it because I never run track before but I knew I was athletic. But I started to move up real, real fast and the coach started recognizing me; as soon as I tried out they recognize me and then I just move up move up until I was number 1. I had the number 1 spot. And the attention I got from my coaches, him taking me off campus, buying me extra running gear on the side. And the meets I'm going to and then all the other staff that's on campus that knew me from my sports they hear how good I am. It was the attention and the fact that I was doing something I was good at and I really, really liked, that kept me running.

Like many of the young men I interviewed, Connor's mother failed to provide for his basic needs and Connor had to take care of himself from an early age. Money was in short supply. His mother struggled to pay rent and Connor and his siblings moved from place to place. Connor's stepfather was a drug addict who didn't work. From Connor's perspective, he strained the meager financial resources of the family. After his mother had a child with her new partner, Connor and his brother felt she had lost interest in them.

> My mom . . . she made a lot of bad decisions. I'm pretty sure she would have said no, I still love you guys and all that. I believe deep down she probably did, but . . . she would blame us for her stuff being missing. We would know who stole it. We said we didn't steal it. It was actually her boyfriend. She would never believe he stole anything. . . . I was like eleven or twelve. This is like when . . . I started looking back on everything, like alright, I'm done with my mom.

Connor craved the positive attention Glen Mills offered. He loved the school because it allowed him to experience a kind of normalcy, like going to the mall, watching a movie, which middle-class teenagers take for granted. Connor got a glimpse into how life could be if his parents had been more stable. He simply had no incentive to complain about violence that he did not even perceive as being out of the ordinary.

In contrast to Connor, who spent more than twenty-four months in Glen Mills, William was only there for 90 days. Staff members didn't personally beat up William, but he witnessed the escalating violence that took place there:

They got this system, if they feel they need to put hands on somebody, its supposed to be . . . they put their hand on your shoulder, and if you still like acting up and all that then they supposed to restrain you and all that. But they don't follow what they're supposed to do at all. They might choke you, smack you around, hit your head.

On the other hand, William acknowledges that the "hands-on approach" is successful. In comparison to other placements very little fighting happens between youths at Glen Mills: "They don't fight each other up there, 'cause if you get caught fighting, that's when they really start putting fists [on you]."

William also recalls the staff's emotional abuse. In addition to getting beaten up, the youths who got into fights were forced to do chores as a punishment. He remembers, for example, that you might have had to spend your free time sitting back on your hands while kneeling. The staff would also assign a "Lint Picking Hour" during which the student had to crawl on his hands and knees to pick lint off the carpet. I asked him if knows whether or not anyone ever reported this kind of abusive behavior. William believed that some of the juvenile probation officers were aware of what had been happening at Glen Mills: "I don't know if they know the extreme. But they know they be doing way more than they supposed to." He remembers that one student told his PO about the beatings but nothing changed. On the contrary, as William recalls, "they [the staff at Glen Mills] gave him a negative transfer to another unit."

In contrast to William, Robert was at Glen Mills long enough to take full advantage of their vocational programming. He never witnessed someone getting beaten up, but he saw staff "throw somebody through a wall or a table." Robert believes that they "are tough for a reason." He argues it just showed him that he "can't mess up." Very similar to Connor he also praises the opportunities the facility has to offer: "Scholarship-wise," he recalls, "they got almost every vocation up there, almost every sport, they got all that stuff." He is convinced that Glen Mills is a good institution to be in if you are actually trying to do something positive with your life.

Connor, William, and Robert are not condemning the program. They are disturbed by the violence but they are equally swayed by the opportunities the institution provided. Although they voiced their concern about the staff's practices, it never reached the threshold of something they would report, especially given the questionable efficacy of such a complaint.

John is the only former Glen Mills resident I interviewed who could not handle the violence the staff resorted to. Unlike the other respondents, John did not talk about any emotional or physical abuse at home. He remembers that his parents did everything for him and were always involved in his life.

Being at Glen Mills was a shock for him. John was sent to Glen Mills twice. He stayed there in 2010 and 2011. In his opinion "Glen Mills is crazy." The second time around he couldn't finish his time there. "I kept getting in trouble and they just kept putting their hands on me," he says. He came back to the reform school when he violated his probation. As soon as he was back there, he began fighting with the staff. Different than many of the other young men who went through Glen Mills, he did not respond well to the school's extremely authoritarian approach to discipline. John managed to get a transfer after he had stayed there only for a few months.

The emotional and physical abuse the young men experienced at Glen Mills is terrifying on its own account. Even more disturbing is that staff members seem to appeal to dysfunctional and outdated male role behavior in order to cover up their abuse. Staff members found easy victims in the Glen Mills students. In a correctional setting relationships between inmate and staff are always unilateral. Staff has tremendous power over juvenile inmates, and since inmates have nothing to offer in return, staff are able to achieve an interactional advantage (Soyer 2016).

The young men often came from abusive homes. They were already primed to tolerate a high level of violence and they had learned to be suspicious of state institutions. Remaining silent about the staff's abusive transgressions was the obvious choice for them. The abusers also knew how to wield their power. They bribed their victims, teased them with privileges. Insidiously, they counted on the fact that these extremely disadvantaged young men would not want to risk losing out on the opportunities Glen Mills had to offer. The young men themselves could easily fall back on a familiar coping mechanism. Being a man also means being able to take a beating. This hypermasculine atmosphere, combined with the racial and socioeconomic stigma of the young men at Glen Mills, enabled abuse and all but guaranteed that the perpetrators would not face any repercussions.

CONCLUSION

The young men I interviewed constructed a male identity that resonated with Adam Reich's "outsider masculinity." The respondents defined "being a man" in terms of dominance, conspicuous consumption, and the ability to suppress emotions. Manhood also entailed presenting oneself as the caretaker of the family, filling in when fathers and stepfathers failed to step up to the task.

They used their definition of manhood as a justification for the crimes they had committed. Yet, their life histories also reveal that their hypermasculine identity is also a response to the reverse maturity gap (chapter 3), they lived through. Defining themselves as their family's provider offered them the illusion of agency in the face of their parents' inability to provide a stable home. In their minds, they stepped up when mothers were overwhelmed and fathers were incarcerated. Selling drugs, for example, not only afforded them a certain lifestyle, it also covered groceries and rent.

Constructing their identity around traditional masculine roles also increased the young men's vulnerability to physical and emotional abuse or neglect in the different realms of their lives. Based on their rather Darwinistic worldview, submitting to those who are stronger and more powerful, such as their violent stepfathers, or the abusive staff members at Glen Mills, was a normal part of life. Emotional and physical abuse, they believe, strengthens the masculine self. "Crying about it" was not only unmanly, it made things worse.

A majority of the respondents also preferred remaining with their family despite abuse, neglect, and deprivation over the alternative of foster care placement. This mistrust of government agencies was more than confirmed for those six respondents who were admitted to the renowned Glen Mills Schools. The staff's abuse they had to endure was an extension of their victimization at home. Unsurprisingly, John, who grew up with parents who did not resort to physical punishment to discipline their son, was the only one who did not praise the Glen Mills Schools.

The abuse at Glen Mills more than anything symbolizes the broken connection between the state and its poorest citizens. Even in Glen Mills, which represents a costly rehabilitative measure, physical violence is a regular part of life. Almost ironically, this celebrated institution exposes the widening gulf between curated upper-middle-class childhoods and the lives of children who grow up poor (Lareau 2003). As Shamus Khan (2011) shows, privileged teenagers readily embrace the opportunities they are born into. The elite institutions through which they pass affirm that their academic success is due to hard work rather than to the advantages bestowed on them at birth. The young men I interviewed, on the other hand, were so used to being abused and neglected, they were grateful for any opportunity Glen Mills provided despite the rampant abuse.

Government institutions, juvenile placement, reforms schools, and eventually the adult criminal justice system played into the already skewed masculine identity of the young men. The utter lack of autonomy, being forced to take orders from correctional officers, and submitting to a rigid timetable lead some to frame incarceration as the ultimate male experience. They refuse to see themselves as Foucaultian "docile bodies" but want to be perceived as "real men" who can endure any hardship (Foucault 1995). According to the motto "don't do the crime if you can't do the time," the Pine Grove respondents also refuse to assign blame to anyone but themselves (Soyer 2016). Their readiness to take responsibility for their actions, however, may not aid desistance as much as it obscures the systematic neglect and disadvantage the young men experienced over their life-course.

6. Losing Children

Communication between Marc and his family has broken down since his transfer upstate in 2010. When I interviewed his mother and his sister during the fall of 2014, they had never visited him at Pine Grove. His mother had not spoken to him on the phone for a long time either. Marc's most recent letter had been hostile and his mother's reply never reached him. She must have unknowingly violated one of the many rules that apply to sending mail to inmates in state prison. During the interview his sister and I compared our impressions of Marc. I had met a reserved young man whose quietness seemed to border on depression. She remembered her brother as a gregarious teenager. While his sister and I talked about Marc and this apparent change in demeanor, Ms. Francis began crying quietly. We stopped our conversation and I tried to console her as best as I could. I did not know what to say other than that SCI Pine Grove was a well-run prison and that I believed her son was safe.

Initially, I wanted to talk to parents and friends of the Pine Grove inmates to get a more complete image of the young men's lives. My goal was to corroborate some of their narratives and to understand where they came from. When I began interviewing the young men's relatives, I realized that they had a story of their own to tell. Their son's, grandson's, or nephew's criminal behavior and incarceration had caused hardship and pain. Some mothers felt guilty for not having done enough. Others expressed disappointment and frustration because of the sacrifices they had made on behalf of the young men. Ms. Francis, I learned, had not visited her son because she couldn't afford the ten-hour bus ride from Philadelphia to Indiana (a city and county that is part of the Pittsburgh metropolitan area in western Pennsylvania). She couldn't pay for receiving phone calls from prison either.

Marc's absence shapes his family in many different ways. On one hand, he had been a challenging teenager. His mother was not able control his behavior. Marc's disobedience must have been especially stressful for her since she already struggled to keep a roof over her children's heads. Ms. Francis worried about her son being out on the streets and getting hurt. Not having him at home eases the immediate stress of managing a volatile child and certainly relieves financial pressure. Despite Marc's difficult adolescence and the family's financial woes, his absence also takes an emotional toll on his mother. Ms. Francis misses her son and feels guilty for not visiting him, or at least for not trying to write to him more regularly.

Marc's family exemplifies the myriad and often contradicting ways incarceration impacts the lives of those who are left behind. Losing a child to the criminal justice system is painful. For those who have enough money to remain in contact with a prisoner, financial means are stretched to the limits. It is expensive to pay for travel, phone calls, and making sure that the inmate has money in his prison account (Comfort 2008). Families like the Francises, who never had enough money to get by, unwittingly lose contact with their child. They have to deal with the guilt feelings stemming from unreturned phone calls and their inability to follow through on visitations. Although Ms. Francis is concerned about her son's well-being, she also knows that he is safer on the inside than out on the street. When Marc is at SCI Pine Grove, she does not have to worry about him getting beaten up, shot at, or arrested for a crime that may be even worse than the one he had already committed. In her case, having an incarcerated son is simultaneously a relief and a burden.

The interviews I conducted show that each family develops individual coping strategies related to their idiosyncratic social circumstances. At the same time, most family members with whom I spoke agree that incarceration is at best a temporary solution. Just like for the inmate, the real work for the family resumes when a prisoner returns home. Most relatives I met knew from experience that they might be sent into a tailspin of worry, exhaustion, and exasperation yet again, shortly after the former convict reunites with his family.

INCARCERATION AND THE FAMILY

Because of the prohibitive costs of incarcerating more than 2 million Americans, research on mass incarceration and prisoner reentry has garnered attention beyond academia.[1] Early work mostly focuses on the economic impact that incarceration has on the life-course of prisoners (Western 2006).

Ten years after the first studies investigating the effects of mass incarceration on the prisoners' communities, researchers begin to understand the basic contours of how children and partners of the imprisoned fare on the outside.

For better or worse, the criminal justice system touches not only those who have committed a crime but also the inmates' network of family and friends (Comfort 2008; Wakefield and Wildeman 2013). Those who stay in touch with their loved ones, for example, may experience "secondary prisonization," with the criminal justice system becoming a third variable in their relationship (Comfort 2003). We also know that children of incarcerated mothers face a high risk of ending up in foster care (Andersen and Wildeman 2014). Likewise, paternal incarceration increases the odds of a child becoming homeless (Wildeman 2016).

Unsurprisingly, incarceration also has measurable effects on the physical and mental well-being of those who are left behind. Lee, Fang, and Luo (2013) find that both physical and mental health problems (e.g., asthma, depression) during adolescence can be related to having a parent in prison. Daughters of incarcerated parents face an increased risk of becoming obese (Roettger and Boardman 2012); and having an incarcerated partner decreases the mental health of mothers who single-parent their children (Wildeman, Schnittker, and Turney 2012).

Sara Wakefield et al. (2016), however, caution us against drawing simplistic conclusions from what at first sight seem to be unequivocal results. They argue that many of those who are incarcerated were far from being functioning and supportive partners or caregivers when they were on the outside. Losing a family member to jail or prison can have unexpected positive effects on the well-being of inmates' families. As the authors point out, incarceration is more likely to create economic hardship when a caregiver made a significant financial contribution to the family. Megan Comfort's qualitative data indicates exactly that. Comfort (2008) observes that in some cases, women who have suffered through domestic violence perceive their partners' incarceration as a temporary relief.

Nancy Rodriguez (2016) suggests that understanding families as transactional units allows us to uncover the counterintuitive ways incarceration can affect families. Few cases allow for clear-cut judgment. An inmate may have contributed financially to his family but may have been a burden on his partner and children emotionally. An incarcerated father could have struggled with drug addiction but still may have provided sporadic emotional and financial support for his children. According to Rodriguez these ambivalent cases can only be addressed adequately if the complexity of family life at the margins of society is taken seriously.

To get a better understanding of how families cope with the incarceration of a child I spoke to caregivers or close relatives of twenty-one of the thirty young men I interviewed in Pine Grove. The missing data is not random. Some parents had already cut ties to their adolescent sons long before they had arrived at Pine Grove and those parents were particularly difficult to track down. In most cases I was not able to locate them. The data are therefore skewed toward those families that are willing and able stay in touch with an incarcerated relative through phone calls and visitation.[2] With this caveat in mind, I propose to treat the data as a limited qualitative insight into the family dynamics that can unfold when a child is incarcerated.

GOOD PEOPLE

Alexander's parents are supportive and engaged. They can afford to visit him regularly and are able to support him financially. "They are really good people," he says. Even though he has done "some messed-up things," they have always been by his side. Alexander was born in in Venezuela. His parents adopted him and his two siblings when he was three years old. Before Alexander and his siblings were put on a flight to the United States to meet their new parents, they lived in an orphanage. The conditions there were horrific. Alexander does not remember a lot about his early years, but recalls that the orphanage was a "really messed-up" place. There was not enough food. He remembers touching a car that belonged to one of the women who worked there. As a punishment she cut part of his thumb off. Alexander has been diagnosed with PTSD and reactive attachment disorder. The scars of the physical and mental pain he experienced will stay with him for the rest of his life.

When I asked Alexander about contacting his parents, he warned me that they are reclusive and may not feel comfortable doing an interview. I had only reached their answering machine but I decided to stop by their house anyway, to see if somebody was home. Alexander's parents live in a middle-class neighborhood. I was lucky and Alexander's mother was at home. Ms. Muniz agreed to speak to me but only if I didn't tape our interview because she believes that her voice sounds "funny" on tape. I was allowed to take notes on my computer during the interview.[3]

Alexander's mother confirms that the first years of Alexander's life were horrific. She knows that the siblings were abused and all three of them were malnourished when they arrived in the United States. Ms. Muniz and her husband are both social workers and they thought that they were well prepared to deal with children who had been traumatized. In hindsight she explains that both of them underestimated the challenges their children faced. Not only were they working through their brutal early childhoods, but they also had to find their way in a strange, new country whose language they didn't know.

Alexander has mostly relied on the recollections of his older sister and maybe even a certain amount of imagination to reconstruct where he comes from. He claims his father was involved in the drug trade. He says that he and his older brother witnessed his father getting shot. They watched him die while they were hiding. Back then he explains the different cartels were fighting to fill the power vacuum left by Pablo Escobar's death. Apparently, his biological mother and his oldest brother were killed shortly after his father's murder.

Alexander read up on the history of the Columbian drug cartels and constructed his identity around it. His uncle, he says not without admiration, was leading one of the cartels. Alexander's mother explains that this idea of his uncle as a high-profile drug boss may be fabricated. She speculates that his sister could have told him something like that or he may have heard a similar story at the orphanage. Either way, the idea of having had a powerful and dangerous uncle fit into the persona Alexander tried to project. His mother remembers that his classmates were racist. They made fun of his Latino background. Ms. Muniz believes he wanted to be seen as a tough guy so that the other students would leave him alone.

As the oldest, Alexander's sister initially struggled the most to transition from an abusive orphanage to an American suburban home. She has been institutionalized for years because of her mental health problems. Alexander was held back in first grade. His mother believes that being deprived of food during his early childhood may have negatively impacted his cognitive development. Ms. Muniz recalls that Alexander couldn't sit still and struggled when learning how to read. Unfortunately, she remembers, he did not have many teachers who were willing or able to work with him creatively.

His behavior became worse in seventh grade when peer pressure increased. During eighth and ninth grades his mother felt she couldn't control him anymore. He started doing drugs and moved out of his parent's house to live with another teenager who stayed by himself. Finally, his parents managed to get Alexander into a residential treatment facility to address his mental health problems. Unfortunately, he acted out violently and was not allowed to remain there.

Alexander's behavior deteriorated when his father was diagnosed with cancer. Alexander remembers that he was extremely scared he would lose another parent. He explains: "I put up my defenses and I just . . . started being a jerk." His mother recalls what happens when Alexander acts like a "jerk." Once he ran away from a residential facility, got drunk, stole a car, and drove it into a light pole. Another time, he had a home pass and stayed with his family overnight. When everybody else was asleep he left. He again stole a car, this time from another teenager he didn't like, and drove all the way to Ohio. In the end he called his parents to tell them where he had gone. His father drove to Ohio to pick him up and Alexander turned himself in.

EMOTIONAL RELIEF

After Ms. Muniz has seen Alexander recidivating time and again, she knows his pattern. He usually does well for a few days after he has been released but then, as his mother puts it, his brain gets scattered. The last time he was at home Alexander again seemed to adjust well to living at home. Conflicts arose when Alexander had his girlfriend stay over without his parents' permission. Both parents felt it was inappropriate for her to stay overnight because there were younger foster children in the home. They told Alexander he couldn't stay if he didn't obey their rules and he decided to move in with his girlfriend.

Ms. Muniz says she knew then that it wasn't a good environment for him. His girlfriend had spent time in prison as well. She finally met the girlfriend's mother, after Alexander was arrested yet again for driving a stolen car. Ms. Muniz learned that her son presented himself as someone who was very wealthy. He had told his girlfriend's family that he had paid for his parent's house and claimed to be looking for another residence he and his girlfriend could move into. These delusions, his mother says, show that Alexander struggles with severe mental health issues that have to be addressed if he is ever to live a stable and productive life.

To understand how Alexander's incarceration has impacted his family, we have to focus on his life immediately before he was sent to SCI Pine Grove. Whatever equilibrium the family had achieved was challenged when Alexander's father had to fight a life-threatening illness. Both Alexander and his mother confirm that his behavior got worse when his father was diagnosed with cancer. At the beginning of our conversation Alexander's mother felt uneasy about sharing her side of the story. After our interview Ms. Muniz told me that it was cathartic for her to revisit what had happened.

Alexander's mother suffered emotionally because of her son's repeated arrests and mental health struggles. For her, Alexander's incarceration relieves some of the tension his presence creates in the family home. While she never explicitly talks about feeling guilty, she acknowledges that she and her husband were naïve about the challenges of their newly adopted children. Being away from Alexander is also painful because she knows that being locked up does not help him either. When he is incarcerated she worries about what will happen once he is released again. She explains that Alexander does not transition well into an unstructured social setting. Ms. Muniz believes that every time Alexander recidivates, his chance of living a normal life decreases.

A PROBLEM CHILD

John is a friendly, talkative, and sometimes even self-deprecating mixed-race inmate. His Caucasian mother separated from his African American father when she was pregnant with John. When his maternal grandparents learned that they were going to have a mixed-race grandchild, they distanced themselves from the young family and John's mother had to make it on her own. During his early life his mother's housing situation was very unstable. She and her little boy moved around between friends' houses. Looking back, John's mother believes that the housing instability must have caused a lot of stress for John.

Only when John turned ten and his sister entered in kindergarten did his mother's life become more stable. For the last ten years she has lived in a small row house in Chester. While her house is well maintained, the street John grew up on shows typical signs of urban decay: empty lots, boarded-up houses, and trash littering the sidewalks. When he was ten years old he witnessed one of his friends getting shot accidentally in the head and stomach. He recalls: "It was right at the end of our block, and we all used to go there after school. He [the boy who was shot] was out in the street with us. Maybe somebody was playing with guns, but we wasn't though. The older kids that was the target that day was the ones playing with guns." John says the boy survived but had to wear a colostomy bag.

John remembers that his mother used to call him a "problem child" and he doesn't deny that he caused trouble as soon as he entered elementary school. He remembers that he had to repeat kindergarten: "They hated me," he says, and explains that he was fighting, not listening to the teacher, and didn't do the assigned work. When I ask his mother whether or not the school did enough to help John she assures me that that his elementary school teachers did everything they could to be supportive. He participated in individualized education programs (IEPs). In the end, his mother remembers, "He didn't even stay in school long enough to get a report card." John received counseling for seven years but that also seemed to have a little effect on his behavior.

His actions escalated from disobedience in school to petty crimes. He readily admits: "I was a vicious thief. . . . I would steal and tell them, I swear to God it wasn't me." He believes that he was looking for attention from the adults around him: "It was like people paid attention to me more. Like make sure you do this, sit down, people would always be near me." His mother also describes John as someone who longed for a relationship with his father or grandparents, none of whom played a big part in his early life. She explains that she always felt that as a single mother she couldn't give him the attention he wanted. He was longing for more people to be present in his life.

John became more involved in street life as he entered puberty. His mother believes that he may have been a follower initially but took on more of a leadership role over time. In addition to John his mother has another daughter, who was fifteen when I met her. Her daughter, she says, is very different than John. She is a good student who never causes problems. After praising her daughter John's mother is quick to point out that she loves both of her children. However, she also admits that she cannot live with John over the long term. Ms. Anderson is also forthcoming about the mistakes she made. She especially regrets using physical punishment to discipline John. Nevertheless, she insists that she tried as much as she could to be there for her son.

John echoes her statements. He remembers his mother showing up at school simply to control his behavior. Ms. Anderson had hoped her presence would prevent him from acting out. The family reached a breaking point when John stole money from his mother and was caught trying to break into her place of work. John's mother remembers how angry and humiliated she was: "'I can't take no more, you broke into my job and got caught, you know how embarrassing it is? I gotta tell them it was my son that did it. That was crazy."

Another time John took her money access card that had $2,400 on it. He spent it over the course of several days. After this incident she kicked him out of the house. John, about thirteen years old, then went to live with his father after this incident. His mother remembers that from that age on he spent a lot of time in juvenile placement.

Ms. Anderson has observed that John's behavior influences how she parents her daughter. She says that his criminal behavior has made her suspicious of her daughter as well. She tries to yell less at her but she admits that she has struggled to find the right tone because her first instinct is to expect the worst. John's mother is proud of her daughter. Her pride, however, reveals even more how ashamed she is of her firstborn. She distinctly remembers a teacher telling her that her daughter "is a pleasure to have in class." This was the first time she remembers that she was able to hold her head high when she was walking a child to school.

ASKING FOR MORE

John's mother does not have a lot of money but she works regularly and her basic needs are met. As a result, John expects financial support from her. Ms. Anderson, however, cannot afford to send him money every time he asks for it. She explains: "He don't understand that I'm broke now. He'll write me four letters a week, send me money, send me money. He's saying send me money, and I didn't even have electric in my house." Unlike Ms. Francis, Ms. Anderson stays in touch with her son and her limited financial resources are depleted as a result of it. Making just enough money to be able to offer some support but not enough to meet his needs puts stress on her. For someone in her position a child's incarceration generates more monetary burden than relief. On the other hand, John's absence likely made it easier for her to focus her energy on her daughter. With John away in prison his little sister is also isolated from the repercussions of his criminal behavior.

Similar to Ms. Muniz, John's mother is also worried about what happens when John gets released. Most of all she wants to move to a different neighborhood. "It's not safe for him here," she says. His impending release therefore creates pressure for her to find a new home quickly. She is also afraid that he has not changed at all during his time at SCI Pine Grove. "I want him to come home and do the right things, but I'm scared that he's not," she explains. Ms. Anderson is not only worried about her son's recidivism but his general ability to live an independent life. His mother worries that John will end up being institutionalized for the rest of his life. She is afraid that he does not know how to act in ways that are socially acceptable because he has already spent so many years in juvenile placement or prison.

Like Ms. Muniz she anticipates another cycle of recidivism to ensue once her son returns. While she may not feel "secondary imprisonization," she is aware that her son does not receive the help he needs and by extension her family will continue to bear the burden of her son's actions. She repeatedly mentions that she just does not know what is wrong with him: "Sometimes," she says, "I think, . . . he doesn't feel stuff the way we feel it. When he does something wrong, I don't, I don't see him sad or thinking, oh, I did something wrong, I'm not gonna do it again. I never see that, never."

"WHEN BLACK WAS NOT BEAUTIFUL"

Jeremiah's grandmother is a charismatic, dark-skinned black woman. She takes pride in her spotless and carefully furnished home. Already in her late sixties her appearance projects the habitus of an upper-middle-class woman. Ms. Thompson grew up during a time when moving up the social ladder was almost impossible for black women. "I lived in an era when black was not beautiful," she remembers. Her short fuzzy hair, she says, was "another strike [against me], it was called a pepper head." As a child she learned that her dark skin color was undesirable, even in comparison to other African American children. She explains:

> I tried to get on the merry-go-round if my grandmother gave me the nickel, and the man would pick all the children around me. Many of them were black, but they were light, light, and I didn't know why I couldn't ride the merry-go-round. I was holding my hand up very high to show him that I had the coin, and he never gave me a ride. Never.

Ms. Thompson says she refuses to be defeated, even when she faces uphill battles. She has been a foster mother for decades and augments her income with a small catering business she runs out of her kitchen. Her grandson, she insists, comes from a good home: "He can't say he didn't know . . . he had a good foundation." Ms. Thompson wanted her children to have a better life. One of her daughters, Ms. Lewis, graduated college from Villanova and now resides in a wealthy suburb of Chicago with her husband and her two children. Jeremiah's mother has always been the exact opposite of her striving sister. She has been struggling with drug addiction since high school. At one point she managed to stay clean for five years. When I interviewed Ms. Thompson, her daughter was trying again to live without drugs. Her mother is skeptical of her daughter's chances to stay clean. She has witnessed her daughter relapse too many times.

Over the past decades the open discrimination of Ms. Thompson's youth has become socially unacceptable. Her grandson's incarceration, however, is a reminder of her precarious social status as an African American woman. When she visits Jeremiah, correctional officers assume that she is guilty by association and treat her accordingly. Again, she is waiting in line, at the mercy of others; and again, somebody may deny her access without having to give her a reason.

Ms. Thompson remembers times when she spent a total of twelve hours on a bus in a single day—six hours to SCI Pine Grove and six hours home—and did not end up seeing Jeremiah because she was told he was in the infirmary or had landed in the segregated housing unit. Like every visitor she is subject to the clothing restrictions and searches before she is allowed to enter. Even Jeremiah's six-year-old niece was not allowed to enter with a sleeveless jumper.

Ms. Thompson tries to practice detachment from the process and attempts to take the perspective of the correctional officers. She explains that being suspicious is part of their job. She remembers that a woman tried to smuggle cocaine in her baby's diaper when they were visiting, but she feels judged and penalized for visiting her grandson nevertheless. One time she recalls that the bus for her return trip back to Philadelphia was late. The correctional officers made people wait on an unlit road in front of the prison. She remembers thinking, "My god, we haven't done anything. Why would you put us out into a dark road?"

BETWEEN FEAR AND ACCEPTANCE

Ms. Thompson has just enough money to pay for the trips and accept her grandson's phone calls. "He's run my bill up $300 in one month for phone calls, which I cannot afford." She tries to make it work regardless. "I cannot afford to cut the communication off because he needs me," she explains. Staying in touch with Jeremiah has put her into a financially precarious situation. She also knows that her grandson does not do well in an institutionalized environment. Ms. Thompson believes that her grandson is at risk of getting hurt or hurting himself while he is incarcerated. She knows her grandson is afraid to eat lunch and dinner with the other inmates because fights break out. He also told her that he stays in his cell because he is terrified of the other inmates. She worries about him skipping meals because he is underweight already. Over the past few weeks, she has been more concerned about his well-being than usual. Ms. Thompson explains that Jeremiah's stress level is "through the roof" because his parole board meeting is coming up. She feels powerless in the face of her grandson's struggles: "It just tears me up. I can't do nothing, and I have to accept that."

Jeremiah's grandmother has been heavily invested in his upbringing. Together with Ms. Lewis she has tried to compensate for her other daughter's inability to be a stable presence in her children's lives. Ms. Thompson took custody of her grandchildren and sent Jeremiah and his sister to a private Catholic school. She has always been aware of his educational challenges and tried to find a setting that would cater to his needs. His sister also struggled in a regular classroom, and Ms. Thompson enrolled her in a specialized private Quaker school. Ms. Thompson always thought that vocational training would be the right choice for Jeremiah, but his reading skills were too weak to finish training as an electrician. His self-esteem plummeted and his grandmother believes that he turned to gang-involved friends to rebuild his self-confidence.

FINANCIAL AND EMOTIONAL COSTS

Each caregiver grappled with specific socioeconomic and emotional constellations that shaped how their son's or grandson's incarceration impacted them. Ms. Muniz, for example, knows that her son does reasonably well when he is incarcerated. Unlike Ms. Thompson she does not worry about Alexander being victimized while he is in prison.

In contrast to the other parents in this chapter, Ms. Francis is not able to visit her son. She feels guilty for not staying in touch with him. She worries because she has no idea how he is doing and what kind of person he has become over the many years he has been away. Jeremiah's grandmother, on the other hand, makes just enough money to visit her grandson and to pay for his almost daily phone calls. She also sends him a letter every day through "jay pay," which charges a fee to deliver a printed-out email message to inmates. Because she interacts with the Pennsylvania criminal justice system regularly, Ms. Thompson experiences "secondary prisonization" more intensely than the other caregivers (Comfort 2003).

The families' responses to incarceration are individualized but they all share similar worries about the reentry process. Just like Ms. Muniz and Ms. Anderson, Jeremiah's grandmother tries to be prepared for Jeremiah's eventual return. Ms. Thompson does not want him to come back to Philadelphia. Ideally she wants him to live in a rural setting. She believes he would do well working with his hands, maybe living on a farm tending to animals. Jeremiah, she explains, has a lot in common with his grandfather, her husband, who did not know how to read and write either. Her husband made money doing manual labor without a formal education. She hopes that she can find a place for Jeremiah that would allow him to learn hands-on rather than from books. Worrying about Jeremiah's return and possible recidivism overwhelms her. As a Catholic she draws strength from her Catholic faith. "When I think my life is caving in, it reminds me of who I really am. I'm simply a servant," she says.

CONCLUSION

In this chapter I have turned my attention away from the life-course histories of the SCI Pine Grove inmates and focused on the narratives of their caregivers. The families I have met over the course of my research confirm that incarceration impacts each family in idiosyncratic ways. Whether or not incarceration of a child is disruptive or provides a limited form of emotional or financial relief depends on the inmates' position in his family. Secondary prisonization, in particular, is connected to the ability and willingness of family members to stay in touch with an inmate (Wakefield 2016; Rodriguez 2016).

The young men I interviewed hardly had a stabilizing effect on their families when they were on the outside. The respondents were teenagers and they were not legally employed in the months before their incarceration. Overall, the young men's criminal behavior amplified their families' financial and emotional woes. Incarceration, on the other hand, had a mixed effect. For families like the Francises the direct financial costs of incarceration are low because they can't afford to see Marc or speak to him on the phone. Not having to worry about supporting his daily needs is likely a financial relief for his mother.

Ms. Thompson's interview reveals the ways in which incarceration can turn into a financial liability for families. The costs for phone calls, emails, and visitation build up over time. They are a significant burden for those who make just enough to pay for the additional expenses but not enough to do so without risking the family's financial safety.

Likewise, a family's emotional burden also depends on whether or not family members maintain regular contact with a prisoner. Ms. Thompson regularly has to live through humiliating interactions with the criminal justice system. She is attuned to her grandson's struggle but remains helpless. The Francis family avoids secondary prisonization, but Marc's mother has to live with not knowing how her son is faring. She struggles with guilt feelings about being unable to overcome her significant financial constraints.

Alexander's and John's mothers find their sons' incarceration less worrisome than trying to prepare for their impending return. Both young men have been through several cycles of recidivism. Both of them also do well when they are incarcerated. Ms. Muniz and Ms. Anderson may, in fact, carry the least emotional burden of incarceration. Their sons are used to being institutionalized and their requests for support are less urgent than, for example, Jeremiah's. The cases of Ms. Anderson and Ms. Muniz demonstrate that families may feel temporarily relief when an erratic teenager is removed from the household.

Both mothers emphasize, however, that incarceration is unlikely to deter their sons' future criminal behavior. Ms. Anderson and Ms. Muniz are aware that prison time may well be followed by even more risk-taking behavior once their sons are released. Both mothers are also afraid that Alexander and John no longer know how to live outside of criminal justice institutions. For those two mothers the incarceration of their sons is a zero-sum game. It may bring temporary relief, but it is also paired with intense worry and even hopelessness about what will happen once their children return home.

This chapter unequivocally demonstrates that struggling families need more nonpunitive, easily accessible social services. Like the young men, their caregivers are victims of a dismantled social welfare system that did little to ease their financial and emotional struggles. Instead it was the juvenile justice system that fulfilled the educational, physical, and mental health needs of their sons (Soyer 2016). Advocating for more investment in nonpunitive social services may sound utopian in the current political climate. Yet, when mothers are forced to find solace in knowing that their children are safe in a prison cell rather than out on the streets, it is clear that reforming the current punishment and welfare regime should become a political priority.

Conclusion and Policy Implications

Over the course of this book I have argued that the young men I interviewed were caught in a web of poverty and trauma that significantly shaped their pathways into criminal behavior. The kind of adversity they confronted made it almost impossible for them to develop reasonable assumptions about violence, drug use, and criminal behavior in general. While the data I have presented do not allow for simplistic causal arguments about the relationship between poverty and crime, the narratives that have unfolded over the past six chapters reveal that the young men's criminal behavior has to be contextualized within the significant childhood adversity they lived through.

I maintain that the absence of a comprehensive welfare system allowed poverty to reach extreme proportions, and growing up poor impacted the young men's criminal trajectories in multiple ways:

1) Children who faced extreme poverty started their criminal career at a young age with petty crimes. From the respondents' perspective their actions were justifiable because they were driven by an acute need—often for food or clothing.

2) The poverty the young men grew up around increased the likelihood of traumatic experiences, such as going hungry, witnessing gun violence, or losing a caregiver to drugs or incarceration.

3) The absence of an easily accessible, centralized social service system left the young men's mental health needs unaddressed. As a result, the trauma they lived through could deliver its full negative impact on their behavioral adjustment.

4) When their parents failed to make ends meet, the young men faced an acute reverse maturity gap. The respondents took on adult roles before they were physically, cognitively, and emotionally ready to do so. They lived independently and largely without any adult supervision, which in turn opened up more opportunities for criminal behavior.

5) This role reversal between parents and children fed into a hypermasculine identity that not only justified victimizing others, but also made the young men more susceptible to letting their own victimization go unreported.

6) The autonomy to which they became accustomed may have made it difficult for them to respond effectively to juvenile justice programs. Once the young men were used to taking care of themselves, they struggled to adjust to rigid juvenile justice interventions.

The most significant overlap among the respondents' narratives is the early childhood trauma they lived through. These traumatic events were closely connected to the extreme poverty their families lived in. Especially parents who struggled with drug addiction failed to fulfill their children's basic needs. To make matters worse, the young men avoided disclosing any information about their personal situation to outsiders. They feared being in foster care more than living in an abusive household.

The respondents and their caregivers did not have easy access to any nonpunitive governmental social services. Admittedly, it seems comparatively easy to apply for food stamps (SNAP) and Temporary Assistance for Needy Families in Pennsylvania (TANF). The Department of Human Services offers online applications for SNAP and TANF. Caregivers can fill out an application on a computer in any public library. Yet, even in the best-case scenario, when a family is eligible for both TANF and SNAP, the government offers vanishingly little support. The maximum benefit a family of three living in Philadelphia County in 2017 could draw was $907 ($403 in TANF and $504 in food stamps).[1] According to the website of the Philadelphia Housing Authority, the waitlist for subsidized public housing (Section 8) is closed. Consequently, TANF checks also have to pay for market-rate rent; the $403 amount fails to cover even half of Philadelphia's median rent.[2]

Any other assistance a family might be able to receive has to be cobbled together from temporary government programs and nongovernmental welfare providers, such as food or clothing banks.[3] Navigating a decentralized web of organizations can be challenging, especially for those who are struggling to find steady employment in the first place. The same obstacles—mental or physical health problems—that thwart people's participation in the workforce likely also prevent them from maximizing welfare benefits.

As chapter 6 shows, the criminal justice system fulfills some caretaking functions and may provide a temporary reprieve for struggling families. Some parents indicate that knowing their son is held in a controlled and safe environment is a momentary relief from worrying about him. Yet, even in the cases where children adjust well to prison, it is apparent to their caregivers that incarceration does not solve any underlying psychological and behavioral challenges.

AN UNCERTAIN FUTURE

Most of the young men I interviewed were toddlers in the mid-1990s. Looking at my young children today, I try to imagine my respondents as typical, stubborn, yet intensely joyful two or three year olds. Like any young child they must have been eager to explore the world—not knowing that American society had already turned its back on them. When welfare ended and mass incarceration geared up, it became all too easy to withdraw support from struggling families and write their children off as violent and incorrigible.

As a white, well-educated woman of European descent, I have found the United States to truly be the land of opportunity. The education I received at the University of Chicago was better than anything Germany would have had to offer. My children are American and we feel at home in what I believe is the greatest city in the world—New York. The thirty young men at Pine Grove spent their whole life in the United States and never had a chance to participate in the American Dream. They are part of a generation that fell victim to two of the biggest follies of twentieth-century policy: a baseless moral panic about juvenile crime and the dismantling of the welfare system.

About a year after I finished the data collection at SCI Pine Grove, I began participating in data collection for another study about inmate networks. For this research we surveyed inmates who were incarcerated in a relatively open "honor block" at an adult facility in Pennsylvania. A handful of those we interviewed were "lifers" who had already spent decades in prison. For those sentenced to life the unit had become their home. One of them, a black inmate, knew how to draw portraits. The correctional officers and counselors appreciated his work and he had painted a mural of the former Penn State football coach Joe Paterno on one of the office walls.

Younger inmates looked up to him because of the institutional knowledge he had accumulated over decades. While he no longer had any meaningful connections to the outside world, he did play an important role in the ecosystem of this unit (Kreager et al. 2017). He had also found a way to express himself creatively. Through his art he was able to exercise a minimal amount of agency in this highly restrictive environment.

After I interviewed him, it felt as if I had been allowed a glimpse into the future of some of the Pine Grove respondents. For those young men who serve long sentences, being incarcerated in a relatively open unit and finding a small way to express their humanity may be the best they can hope for. Marc, for instance, entered SCI Pine Grove when he was fifteen. Seven years later, he is still incarcerated and has already spent a third of his life in state prison. On the outside he never had a stable place to live. He has lived at SCI Pine Grove longer than at any other house or apartment on the outside.

Publicly available data show that even those respondents who are released will likely return to prison. Since 2014 twenty-five respondents have been released. At the time of this writing thirteen of them are in custody again. One, William, is on the run. Three participants, Henry, Miguel, and Jeremiah, are held in county jails. Eleven have returned to the Pennsylvania state prison system. Another eleven young men are on the outside but remain under parole supervision. In two cases I was not able to verify their current custody status. One of them, Kayden, had been rearrested but was released by court order from county jail. Four respondents, Dylan, Robert, Isaac, and Marc, continue to serve their long sentences. The most significant change in their status has been an official integration into the adult population of the Pennsylvania prison system. They "graduated" from the YAO program and have been transferred to different penitentiaries across the state.[4]

POLICY IMPLICATIONS

State governments allocate a significant amount of money to keeping people behind bars. In 2010 Pennsylvania spent almost $33,000 per inmate over the course of the fiscal year. It was the same year that Marc entered SCI Pine Grove. In 2013 the median income in the census tract Marc lived in at the time of his arrest was $22,712.

Facing these steep costs politicians of both parties agree that incarceration rates must be further reduced (Clear and Frost 2013). It is less clear, however, which reform strategies hold the most promise for preventing recidivism and addressing racial disparities in incarceration. In the search for alternatives, journalists and criminal justice professionals look to coun-

TABLE 6: Current Custody Status

Name	Race	Year of Birth	Conviction
Alexander*	Latino	1993	State Prison
Andrew*	Mixed	1993	State Prison
Austin	Black	1994	Paroled
Blake*	Black	1992	State Prison
Bryan	Black	1993	Paroled
Connor	Mixed	1994	Paroled
Dylan**	Black	1993	State Prison
Elijah	Black	1992	Unknown
Gabriel	Black	1993	Paroled
Henry*	White	1994	County Jail
Isaac**	Black	1994	State Prison
Jaxon*	Black	1994	State Prison
Jeremiah*	Black	1993	County Jail
Jesus*	Latino	1994	State Prison
John	Mixed	1994	Paroled
Jordan	Black	1993	State Prison
Joshua*	Black	1993	State Prison
Josiah*	Black	1993	State Prison
Julian	White	1992	Paroled
Kayden	Black	1994	Unknown
Luke*	White	1994	State Prison
Marc**	Black	1994	State Prison
Mateo	Latino	1993	Paroled
Miguel*	Latino	1992	State Prison
Nate	Asian	1993	Paroled
Oliver	White	1994	Paroled
Robert**	White	1993	State Prison
Samuel	Black	1994	Paroled
Tyler*	Black	1992	State Prison
William*	White	1994	Absconded

* Indicates respondent recidivated.
** Indicates respondent still serving the original sentence.

tries such as Germany, the Netherlands, and Great Britain to find solutions for the overburdened U.S. criminal justice system (Turner and Travis 2015).

In Germany a prisoner sentenced to life is likely going to leave prison after fifteen years. The age of criminal responsibility is fourteen; and the juvenile justice system may be applicable to youths as old as twenty if his or her cognitive maturation is delayed. This rehabilitation-focused penal regime in Germany developed in opposition to the atrocities of the Third Reich. In 1949, when Germany received its new constitution, the Allied Forces, particularly the United States, ensured the creation of a political structure that prevented a recurrence of an inhumane dictatorship. The German Basic Law introduces the concept of inviolable human dignity that has to be protected by all state authority. The German criminal justice system is bound to protect the "human dignity" of its inmates—a much stronger mandate than the protection from cruel and unusual punishment the U.S. Constitution provides.

As important as more humane conditions and shorter sentences are, the biggest difference between Germany and the United States is the presence of an encompassing welfare state. The German equivalent to TANF has no time limit and secures the basic well-being of those who are unemployed. As in the United States, support is tied to household size. Families with children receive more money than a single person. The government covers rent, heat, kitchen utensils, and clothes as well as furniture for the apartment. Additionally, people on welfare receive monetary payments that cover their living expenses. A single mother with two children between the ages of six and fourteen receives 404 euros every month for herself and 270 euros for each child. Her total in-cash benefits are 944 euros (approximately $1,150) monthly *without* having to pay for housing, heating, or clothes.[5] As a brief reminder, the same mother living in Pennsylvania receives $907 ($403 in TANF and $504 in food stamps) to pay for all of her expenses *including* rent, heating, and clothes.

Unsurprisingly, poverty in Germany does not reach the level of desperation the young men recalled in this book. The enormous costs of the German welfare state are forwarded to the German taxpayers. An average family with two children pays 34 percent of their gross income in taxes. The average single person transfers half of their paycheck (49.4 percent) to the government.[6] Such extensive taxes are unthinkable for most Americans. A welfare state such as in Sweden, Germany, and the Netherlands seems therefore unattainable for the United States.[7]

In *Hillbilly Elegy*, a currently popular book about the troubles of an Appalachian upbringing, J.D. Vance recognizes the abysmal disadvantage poor children face. In striking contrast to most children in such a situation,

Vance made it out, became a successful lawyer, and is now a bestselling author. He believes that the loving presence of his grandparents, as well as enlisting in the Marines, taught him the life skills he needed to become upwardly mobile. Vance (2016: 255) vehemently argues that "public policy can help," but that no government can ultimately fix what he perceives as the self-destructive tendencies of the poor. Books like *Hillbilly Elegy* cement the impression that poverty is a self-inflicted wound, and a moral failing rather than a structural problem of extreme inequality.

If the enthusiastic reception of a book like *Hillbilly Elegy* is any indication, it is unlikely that the American public is going to embrace the development of a comprehensive welfare system any time soon. I therefore limit my policy suggestions to what I believe is the most striking paradox of the data I present. The respondents confirmed children in poor communities learn from an early age to circumvent the exact institution that is supposed to protect them. The young men had internalized that child protective services are to be avoided at all costs. They believed that being sent to foster care was worse than staying in their abusive home, and they learned how to hide or explain away their bruises. As a result, the reality of intra-familial violence, as well as the true level of poverty and desperation, remained largely unacknowledged. Furthermore, those who were supposed to rehabilitate the young men did not have access to relevant information about their clients' pasts.

This tragic disconnect between the intention of a government institution like child protective services and the reception by the community is an opportunity to reconsider how the American government serves vulnerable children. Providing support to struggling families without the imminent danger of losing parental rights is crucial for addressing the abject poverty many of the respondents recalled. The German government offers a blueprint for how family services can be structured to support mothers rather than punishing them for their parenting mistakes. In Germany families who struggle with mental illness, physical illness, or are overwhelmed by their child's behavioral issues have access to a "family helper." Those "helpers" are social workers offering temporary assistance. The aim of these social workers is not to remove children from their families; in fact, their service is intended to prevent the removal of children from their home. These social workers are embedded in the family they serve. They teach families how to budget, address children's educational issues, and provide emotional support. The goal is to ensure that children live in a healthy environment that enables their growth and full participation in society.[8] It is not difficult to imagine what a difference such a nonpunitive assistance could have made for the respondents and their families.

In ending this book I would like to return to John Stuart Mill's quote I introduced in the first chapter. The entire passage reads:

> The only freedom which deserves the name, is that of pursuing our own good in our own way, so long as we do not attempt to deprive others of theirs, or impede their efforts to obtain it. Each is the proper guardian of his own health, whether bodily, *or* mental and spiritual. Mankind are greater gainers by suffering each other to live as seems good to themselves, than by compelling each to live as seems good to the rest (1978: 12; emphasis in original).

Over the past decades the U.S. political system has utilized the pretext of protecting individual freedom to systematically ostracize and deprive its poorest citizens of access to the most basic social support. It seems as if American society has internalized Mill's philosophy without accounting for his most crucial caveat: "so long as we do not attempt to deprive others." The current hypercapitalist economy does exactly that—it deprives disadvantaged families and by extension their children of being able to live up to their potential. The young men I portray in *Lost Childhoods* were born just as welfare reform took effect. The government's unwillingness to support their families significantly diminished their ability to make decisions freely without being constrained by the extreme economic hardship their families faced. Paradoxically, their current freedom continues to be curtailed because of the government's eagerness to spent tens of thousands of dollars every year on their incarceration.

Conceptually, it is relatively easy to understand how a racially biased criminal justice system defies core American principles like equality and freedom. Taxing the wealthy to redistribute income, on the other hand, seems be at odds with these core American values. More than a century ago Max Weber described capitalism in the United States as a "sporting contest" completely devoid of "metaphysical significance" ([1904–5] 2002: 121). The young men at the center of *Lost Childhoods* were barely out of the starting block when they already faced significant hurdles. The families I met were enmeshed in a wide range of social ills that made it difficult to provide a healthy and safe environment for their children. *Lost Childhoods* shows that neglecting the weakest members of American society fosters the kind of abject poverty that curtails individual freedom and infringes on basic human dignity. If U.S. society wants to ensure freedom for all its citizens, ending mass incarceration and rebuilding the welfare system is indeed the most important social political goal in the decades to come.

Methodological Reflections

1. ECONOMIC AND SOCIAL CAPITAL IN THE RESEARCH PROCESS

When I started this project I applied for multiple grants and, as is par for the course, I was turned down by most of them. One reviewer doubted that the project was feasible, arguing that it was unlikely I would obtain access to the population I intended to interview. This reviewer was right to be skeptical. My dissertation research taught me that accessing any correctional population is extremely labor-intensive. It can take many months to pass the different Institutional Review Boards (IRBs) involved. Prisoners are considered to be a protected population, and anyone doing research with inmates has to go through an extensive, time-intensive IRB review.

The short time between research proposal and actual data collection for *Lost Childhoods* is a testament to the extraordinary openness of PADOC to research. Being at the Justice Center for Research at Pennsylvania State University had placed me in the fortunate position to have a mentor, Gary Zajac, who had been director of research at PADOC before he joined the faculty at Penn State. He guided me through the process, knowing who to call and how to formulate my requests. Without his help it would not have been possible to finish this study during my two-year tenure as a postdoctoral scholar. I was also extremely lucky to encounter an IRB review board at Penn State University that recognized the value of my work and required very few changes to my research protocol. The quick turnaround between data collection to the publication of this book became possible because the Justice Center for Research supported my work by employing a graduate student who transcribed the data as I was conducting interviews at SCI Pine Grove.

Comparing the fieldwork I did while at Penn State to the data collection for my dissertation exemplifies the difference that financial support makes for research productivity and efficiency. My dissertation research was on the verge of collapse multiple times. I lacked both sufficient financial means and institutional support for the work I was doing. The research for *Lost Childhoods* unfolded in the exact opposite way. My experience demystifies the lore of the lone qualitative researcher who must make tremendous personal sacrifices to collect their data under the most challenging circumstances. More resources not only speed up the research process, they allow for higher-quality data collection and encourage a faster turnaround between data collection and analysis.

It is difficult for qualitative researchers outside of a select few elite institutions to get the kind of support I was fortunate to receive. Increasing the visibility of qualitative research in criminology is only possible if the discipline reconsiders its funding priorities and acknowledges the value of high-quality and up-to-date qualitative work.

2. STUDY DESIGN

Lost Childhoods relies on life-course interviews with thirty young men who were adjudicated as adults as well as face-to-face and phone interviews with their relatives and friends. I met with all but one inmate three times over the course of three months from April to June 2014 at SCI Pine Grove.[1] I recruited inmates through an internal communication system that sent a digital call for participation to those inmates who had a TV in their cell.[2] The interviews were transcribed and inductively analyzed in a word processing program (Glaser and Strauss 2009).

As I briefly elaborated in the book's introduction, I asked the respondents to provide information about a relative or friend who would be willing to participate in an interview. I was able to interview friends, caregivers, or siblings of twenty-four respondents. In six cases I could not locate anyone willing to participate in an interview. The total number of caregiver, sibling, and friend interviews is thirty-one. In seven cases I interviewed two of the respondent's relatives. The total number of interviews conducted for this study is 120.

The convenience sample, as well as the lack of a counterfactual group, may be considered a weakness of this study design. The goal of this study, however, was not to create a representative sample of prisoners in Pennsylvania, or even a representative sample of juveniles adjudicated as adults. I designed the study to access the subjective life-course histories of young men who represent the most difficult cases of the criminal justice system in Pennsylvania. The data should be understood as a Weberian ideal type that allows me to investigate social processes likely obscured in large-scale quantitative studies (Weber 1949). Assuming "historical specific" instead of linear causality, the results of this case study generate new conclusions to be tested in future research. Thus, in aggregate, qualitative case studies such as the present one may lead to a valid theoretical understanding that transcends the specific group of inmates I interviewed (Burawoy 1991).

3. STRENGTH AND WEAKNESS OF INTERVIEW STUDIES

The biggest strength of ethnography is the ability to observe action rather than relying on respondents' recollections. Narrative data are always subjective accountings of events and need to be treated as such (Jerolmack and Khan 2014). On the other hand, retrospective interviews have significant advantages that are more suitable for some research questions. Interviews allow respondents to describe emotions and events in ways only possible after actions and their consequences have fully unfolded.

Most importantly the information I solicited could not be accessed in an ethnographic setting. An ethnographer would likely not witness the kind of extreme abuse the young men described. If he or she did witness such scenes, the ethical responsibility to intervene and report the incidence would prevent any further research from taking place. In that sense, interview data, for all its shortcomings, allows the researcher to access a social reality that most likely would remain hidden otherwise.

4. INTERVIEW PROCESS

Qualitative researchers always have to weigh the depth of data collection with the range of cases they want to capture. In this study I also tried to strike a balance between depth and breadth of data. Talking to thirty respondents is by no means representative, but it allowed me to generate variation in terms of race, class, and the offenses for which the young men were incarcerated. On the other hand, the original group of respondents was still small enough that I could reasonably conduct multiple interviews and meet their families on the outside. All but one respondent allowed me to tape the interviews. In this one case I took notes during and after the interview. The interview guides are attached in Appendix II.

State College where I lived at the time was about a ninety-minute car ride from SCI Pine Grove. To minimize driving back and forth I scheduled up to five interviews a day. At the end of the day, the quality of the interview likely suffered. I made this compromise because my younger daughter was only three months old when I started the interviews and I did not want to leave her overnight. The long days I spent on the unit meant that I became familiar with the correctional officers while also minimizing the institutional burden of repeated visits.

The interview process I experienced was unusually smooth, as I learned later during the data collection for a larger project—the Prison Inmate Network Study. In retrospect I believe the data collection was so efficient because I was the only interviewer. Aside from a small grant from the ASA Fund for Advancement of the Discipline I did not have any funding for my one-woman project. Since I was the only interviewer the study appeared decidedly low-key. Some correctional officers and the respondents, for example, initially thought that I was still an undergraduate working on a class project. While the lack of manpower and financial resources led to compromises such as the long interview days, I was still able to finish the project faster than I had anticipated.

Interviewing respondents more than once was crucial for being able to build rapport and compare the narratives of the young men over multiple sessions. I was also able to clarify aspects of their life-course, especially because most of the respondents recalled a tumultuous back and forth between different homes, alternating caregivers, and rapidly moving in and out of juvenile justice programs.

I also tried to keep the interviews as engaging as possible. To jog their memory I presented different maps of the neighborhood the respondents lived in prior to their arrest. I was able to retrieve that information from their case summary files before our first interview. On the map I had marked their last residence, and where the information was available I also printed out a map of the area in which the young men had committed the crime that led to their adjudication as adults. I started the first interview with simple demographic questions and focused on their current situation as well as their life immediately before their arrest. I also asked them for a detailed recollection of the day that led up to the crime as well as the day they were arrested. I originally intended to focus on the day their crime took place to understand the role of the specific neighborhood characteristics as the interviews progressed; however, this recollection turned into a means of building rapport. The young men recalled their crime and realized that I was not judging them, which in turn increased their willingness to share painful memories about their childhood in the later interviews.

The second interview covered their childhood from birth to twelve years and the third one focused on the teenage years up to the time they came to Pine Grove. The redundancy between the first and third interviews was intentional because it allowed me to ask similar questions after I had built trust with them. In most cases the young men were more forthcoming with information during our second and third meetings. At our last interview Julian admitted that he was much more relaxed than during our first interview.

> It all comes down to comfortability. 'Cause you can make a person comfortable like the way you speak. I mean you speak, when I first met you, like you didn't really speak a lot 'cause you just asked a few questions and then it was over with. But as we talked more and more like now, you cursing with me and everything. It's awesome. You can come here and you can be comfortable. And when you're comfortable with a person, it's easy to talk to them.

Experiencing how multiple interviews increased the quality of the data raises questions about the utility of trying to solicit sensitive information in a single interview. Relying on one meeting with a respondent increases the chance of misrepresentations or misunderstandings. A single interview, therefore, is not likely to result in an adequate representation of the respondent's life-course.

For all of the limits a prison environment places on interviewer and respondent interactions, a prison can also be an ideal setting to conduct an intensive interview study. Being segregated from any outside stimulus encourages respondents to extensively reflect on their pathways into crime. Many inmates welcome a distraction an outside interviewer brings to the unit. As I showed previously, the young men harbored a deep distrust of government representatives, and specifically they did not trust anyone who worked for the Department of Corrections. Thus, while being removed from their usual environment encourages reflection, most respondents did not feel comfortable sharing any of their introspection with the counselors or fellow inmates on their unit.

Since the respondents also self-selected into the study, in many cases the interviews enabled the young men to release built-up tensions. The young men were longing to talk to someone about their past, their current situation, and hopes for the future. I also was a low-risk person to open up to. I had no affiliation with the DOC and no relationship to anyone they knew on the outside. The fact that I am from Germany also peaked the respondents' interest. Another advantage of conducting interviews in the Young

Adult Offender units was that this population, which is difficult to reach on the outside, was readily available for repeated meetings.

5. DATA TRIANGULATION

Not conducting systematic interviews with parents and friends was my biggest regret after my dissertation research about juvenile offenders in Boston and Chicago. Interviewing relatives and friends of the young men was therefore an important aspect of the project from its inception. Those interviews allowed me to gather some observational data about the young men's homes and it increased the confidence I had in analyzing the accounts of the in-prison interviews. In Alexander's case, for example, meeting his mother led me to reevaluate the information he had provided in our interviews and I was able to present the complexity of his case more effectively.

Finally, having access to the case summary files was indispensable for conducting meaningful interviews. It allowed me to prepare the maps that not only made the interviewing process more interesting but also supported the respondents' recollections. The interviews also exposed significant shortcomings of official data. Abuse and neglect was only officially reported in one case. The other young men distrusted representatives of PADOC, and as chapter 5 showed, they also did not necessarily classify their experiences as abuse. The interviews I conducted are a cautionary tale about the shortcomings of the data that criminologists, including myself, rely on regularly to make quantifiable assumptions.

6. DATA INTERPRETATION

In July 1997 I visited the United States for the first time. The trip was organized by my home state, Baden-Württemberg in southern Germany. I was part of a group of high school students who were sent the United States to learn about the American political system. The East Coast cities I visited represented everything the little village I grew up in was not. The politicians and journalists we met in New York City and Washington, DC, celebrated freedom of speech and diversity as core American values. When we toured Capitol Hill I was in awe of the democratic institutions that exuded pride and unapologetic patriotism. The United States symbolized a kind of cosmopolitan society that the Nazis had destroyed in Germany.

Over the past decade I have become disillusioned with the United States. Settling down in the United States for the long term clarified that my daughters will have a very different perception of the role of government than I had growing up in Germany. They will learn that for most Americans getting a higher education means taking on massive debt. They will grow up in a society where good public schools are reserved for people who can afford to pay high property taxes. Eventually my daughters will also understand that having access to good health care is a privilege, not something the government guarantees to everyone.

The arguments I have developed in *Lost Childhoods* reflect my coming to terms with a society I once idealized and now struggle to call home. Max Weber (1949) argues that the causal reality presented by social scientists is always a reflection of values and discourses that dominate the social world the researcher inhabits. An analysis of the social world is only objective insofar as it is contingent on the historical moment the data was collected and analyzed. My analysis is fundamentally shaped by my subjective reaction to the kind of values that are currently pervading American society. Consequently, the conclusions I have drawn are also an outcome of the increased friction between my assumptions about what constitutes a fair and just society and the reality of the country in which I have chosen to raise my children.

In that sense, another researcher, socialized in a different culture, may be able to discern patterns I did not see in the data and may come to conclusions that I could have not drawn. I still maintain that the cultural contingency of interpreting qualitative data is not necessarily a weakness but part of what makes small N studies so valuable for exploratory research and theory building. For me personally, qualitative research is not about finding universal truth. I believe it is the strength of qualitative research that it reveals the extent to which class, race, gender, and, in my case, cultural heritage, matter as we analyze real-world data.

Interview Guides

1. LIFE-COURSE INTERVIEWS: PINE GROVE

Interview 1: Current Situation

Demographics
   Name:
   Date of birth:
   Last address before arrest:
   Number of siblings:
   Age of siblings:
   Number of children:

Background Information
   Where were you born?
   From the earliest time you can remember, how many times did you move to a different place?
   Can you recall the addresses where you lived, from when you were born until your arrest? If you can, put the first address you remember first, etc.
   The respondent will be asked to fill out the following form:

Street Name	*City, State*	*Year lived at address*

   What was the date of your arrest that led you to come here?
   How many times have you been arrested before?
   Were you involved with the juvenile justice system?
   Were you involved with the Pennsylvania's child welfare system?
   What other institutions besides Pine Grove have you been incarcerated in?

How long have you been in Pine Grove?

When will you be released?

Do you have any idea what you will be doing after you get out?

Daily Life in Pine Grove

Tell me about your daily routine here.

- What programs are you enrolled in?
- Can you describe a typical day for me?
- How often do you get visitors?
- What is the hardest thing about being incarcerated?

What is your main source of communication with people on the outside?

How often do you receive letters / phone calls / visits?

Who is the person that you miss most? Why?

Neighborhood / Community

A map will be presented to the respondent that contains his final residential address, the school he attended / place of employment, as well as the place where he committed the crime that led to his arrest. [Information is based on the case files accessed before the first interview.] The respondent will be asked to mark on the map his movements immediately before his arrest.

Can you draw on this map the boundaries of what you would consider to be your neighborhood around the time of your arrest?

Can you tell me what a typical day looked like in the three months before you got arrested:

Where did you spend your days / nights during that time?

Can you retrace the way you typically took to get to school / work?

[Where did you get on the bus / subway?]

Can you show me on this map where you would typically hang out after school / work?

For example if you wanted to play basketball or sports, in general where would you go?

Was there a youth club you went to regularly? Where was it and how often did you go there?

Where would you go if you wanted to buy a beer? How often did you go to this store?

Were there any other stores that you went to frequently?

Can you show me where you would spend your time if you skipped school?

Who was usually with you during that time?

Can you show me on the map where you would meet your friends and which way you would take to get there?

How did your routine change on the weekends?

Where did you spend your days / nights?

What would you do on a typical Saturday or Sunday? Can you point out the places on the map where you would usually be on Saturdays or Sundays?

I would like you to think about the day you got arrested. What do you remember about that day?

- What was your original plan for that day?
- When you left the house, can you retrace the steps to your first destination that day?
- Where did you go after that? [Subway / Bus stop]
- How did your plans change over the course of the day and why?
- Can you show me on this map the last stop you made before you got arrested?

[If inmate does not claim to be innocent] What went through your mind right before you committed your crime?

If you look back to that day, what would you do differently?

Reflection on Crime / Arrest

Why do you think you ended up in Pine Grove?

- How old were you when you first got involved with the streets?
- What was the first crime you committed?
- Do you remember why you did it?
- Who or what do you think is responsible for you being here?
- What could have changed your fate?

Interview 2: Childhood: Age 0–12

The respondent will be shown a map / maps that indicate the different addresses where he has lived. Information about his residential history was gathered during the first interview.

Can you put a number on the different places that you lived at: 1 = first place I remember living, etc.?

The respondent will additionally be asked to fill out the form below to verify his residential history and to fill in some of the missing information.

Residential History age 0–12

Address	Stayed there from XX until XX	People living in the same household	Main care-taker	Kindergarten / Elementary School attended (if you attended several schools while you were living at a specific address, please list all of them)

At which of these places did you stay the longest? For how long did you live there?

Can you write down who lived with you at these different places?

Can you also write down who your main caretaker was when you were living there?

Did you attend preschool or kindergarten?

If yes, can you indicate where on the map your preschool and / or kindergarten was?

Can you point out where you went to elementary school?

Which place did you like best / least? Why?

Family Life

Would you say your mother was an important part of your life then?

- Why? Why not?
- How often did you see her?
- Are you in touch now?
- Did it affect you that she was not a part of your life? How? / Why not?

Would you say your father was an important part of your life?

- Why? Why not?
- How often did you see him?
- Are you in touch now?
- Did it affect you that he was not a part of your life? How? / Why not?

You mentioned that you have XX siblings. Which one of your siblings were you particularly close to before you turned 12 and why?

- Are you still close to him / her now?

What is your first childhood memory?

What is the happiest memory that you have between the ages of 3 and 12? / What were the happiest moments during this time?

If you look back to your childhood, was there anything that you think set you up for ending up at Pine Grove?

What is your most painful childhood memory?

Do you think you were a "problematic" child growing up?

- Why / Why not?

If you could change something about your childhood, what would that be?

Were any of your family members / household members involved in crime / gangs during your childhood?

Yes:

- How do you think that influenced you?

Were any family members / household members addicted to drugs / alcohol while you were a child?

- How do you think that influenced you?

If respondent has children:

- What do you want to do different than your parents raising your child(ren)?

Friends

Respondent will again be shown the map that indicates the residential history. The respondent will be asked to mark specific places that were important during his childhood.

Who were your closest friends during that time?

Can you indicate on your map where your three closest friends lived at the time? Please put initials behind your mark.

How much time did you spend at their houses?

Can you describe what you and your friends would do when you hung out?

Can you indicate on the map the places where you would spent your free time?

Prompt: Youth clubs, basketball court, playground

- Are you still in touch with some of your childhood friends?

Were your friends at the time involved in crime / gangs?

Yes:

- How do you think that influenced you?

Who do you think had more influence on you at the time—your family/siblings or your friends?

Educational Experience

Did you attend preschool/kindergarten?
What do you remember about this time?
What do you remember about elementary school?

- Was there a teacher that you particularly liked?
- What did you not like about school? (teacher, classmates, etc.)

Social Services

Did you work with a social worker/therapist etc. before you turned 12?
Yes:

- What was your experience? (Helpful/not helpful, what did you get out of it?)

Did you take any medicine, for example to deal with depression/ADHD/mood swings during your childhood?
Yes:

- What did you take?
- Who prescribed them?
- Did it help you? Why? /How? /Why not?

Role Models

Was there anyone inside or outside of your family that you looked up to during childhood?
Yes:

- What did you admire about him/her?
- Are you still in touch with this person?
- How do you view him/her differently now?

No:

- Why was that the case?

Interview 3: Adolescence: Age 12 until Arrest

The respondent will be shown a map/maps that indicate the different addresses he has lived at between the ages of 12 until his arrest. Information about his residential history was gathered during the first interview.

The respondent will additionally be asked to fill out the form below to verify his residential history and to fill in some of the missing information.

Residential History age 12—until arrest

Address	Stayed there from XX until XX	People living in the same household	Main caretaker	Middle School / High School attended (if you attended several schools while you were living at a specific address, please list all of them)

At which of these places did you stay the longest? For how long did you live there?

Can you write down who lived with you at these different places?

Can you also write down who your main caretaker was when you were living there?

Which place you lived at did you like best / least? Why?

Can you describe how your life changed as you were growing up and turning into a teenager?

Can you share some of the happiest memories you have from that time?

If you could go back in time, what would you change about your teenage years and why would you change it?

Family Life

Would you say your mother was an important part of your life then?

- Why? Why not?
- How often did you see her?
- Are you in touch now?
- Did it affect you that she was not a part of your life? How? / Why not?

Would you say your father was an important part of your life then?

- Why? Why not?
- How often did you see him?
- Are you in touch now?
- Did it affect you that he was not a part of your life? How? / Why not?

You mentioned that you have XX siblings. Which one of your siblings were you particularly close to after you turned 12 and why?

- Are you still close to him / her now?

What is the happiest memory that you have between the ages of 12 and your arrest? / What were the happiest moments during this time?

If you look back to your teenage years, was there anything that you think set you up for ending up at Pine Grove?

What is your most painful memory from that time?

Do you think you were a "problematic" teenager?

- Why? / Why not?

If you could change something about your teenage years, what would that be?

If respondent has children:

- What do you want to do different than your parents raising your child(ren)?

Were any of your family members / household members involved in crime / gangs during your adolescence?

Yes:

- How do you think that influenced you?

Were any family members / household members addicted to drugs / alcohol while you were a teenager?

- How do you think that influenced you?

Which member of your family / household was most important to you at the time?

- Why?

Friends

Respondent will again be shown the map that indicates his residential history. The respondent will then be asked to mark specific places that were important meeting places for him and his friends during his adolescence.

Who were your closest friends during that time?

Can you indicate on your map where your three closest friends lived at the time? Please put initials behind your mark.

How much time did you spent at their houses?

Can you describe what you and your friends would do when you hung out?

Can you indicate on the map the places you would spent your free time at?

Prompt: Youth clubs, basketball court, playground

- Are you still in touch with some of the friends you had during your teenage years?

Were your friends at the time involved in crime / gangs?
Yes:

•   How do you think that influenced you?

Who do you think had more influence on you at the time—your family / siblings or your friends?
Role Models
Was there anyone inside or outside your family that you looked up to during childhood?
Yes:

•   What did you admire about him / her?
•   Are you still in touch with this person?
•   How do you view him / her differently now?

No:

•   Why was that the case?

Social Services
Where you involved with the juvenile justice system during that time?
Yes:

•   Did you have a probation officer?

Yes:

•   How many different probation officers did you have?
•   How was your relationship with him / her?
•   How often did you meet with him / her?
•   Where would you meet with him / her?
•   Was his / her office close to your home?

Yes: (Take out map.) Can you show me where the office was on this map? Please mark it and write behind the mark how often during one typical week / month you would meet him / her.

•   How would you typically get to the office / the place you would meet him / her? [Prompt what was the bus stop / subway station you used]

How did he / she help you / fail to help you?
Were you incarcerated?
Yes:

•   Where and for how long?
•   How did incarceration help you or fail to help you?

- What other programs were you enrolled in?
- Was there any social worker /probation officer / caseworker that you felt was supportive of you and wanted the best for you?

In your opinion was there anything that the juvenile justice system could have done to help you more effectively?

If you think back to years before you committed the crime that led you here, what could you have done differently?

- Why did you not do it?
- How did you try to get away from the streets or other negative influences?

Were you involved with the Department of Children and Families? Did you have a caseworker?
Yes:

- How was your relationship with him / her?
- How often did you meet with him / her?
- Where would you meet with him / her?
- Was his / her office close to your home?

Yes: (Take out map.) Can you show me where the office was on this map? Please mark it and write behind the mark how often during one typical week / month you would meet him / her.

- How would you typically get to the office / the place you would meet him / her? [Prompt what was the bus stop / subway station you used]
- How did he / she help you / fail to help you?

Was there anything that you wish someone would have offered you that would have prevented you from ending up at Pine Grove?

Educational Experience

Respondent will be shown another map that covers the area he lived in as an adolescent.

Can you indicate where on the map your middle school(s) / high school(s) was (were)? Please indicate the year you attended this school behind the mark you have made.

Can you map for me, for each address you lived at, your way to and from school?

Can you mark the places that you would hang out after school?

If these places changed between age 12 and the time of arrest please indicate the approximate time frame during which you regularly went to this place and how often during the week you would go there. For example: Youth Club X went there from 12–14 every week.

Prompt: Basketball court, youth club, friends' houses

What do you remember about your time in middle school / high school?

- Would you say you attended school regularly?
- Was there a teacher that you particularly liked?
- What did you not like about school? (teacher, classmates, etc.)

Future Plans

Do you know where you are going to move to after you have been released?

How do you want to change your life once you are released? What do you want to do differently than before?

How do you think you can manage to stay out of trouble?

How do you think you can prepare for your life after your release while you are still in here?

2. INTERVIEWS WITH OUTSIDE RESPONDENTS

In addition to the questions below, the interviews will be adjusted individually according to the information gathered from the case summary files and previous interviews with R.

Demographics

Name:

Date of birth:

Relationship to R:

Racial background:

Occupation:

Highest level of education:

Relationship to Original Respondent

If not mother, father, sibling, or other close relative

When was the first time you met R?

How did you meet R?

- How would you describe your relationship to R?
- How close are you?
- Do you trust him? Why? / Why not?
- What do you think are his strengths? What are his weaknesses?

Depending on when he / she met R:

Can you tell me about his early childhood?

- What was he like as a toddler/child?
- How was he different from other children?
- Was he a challenging child? Why?/Why not?
- What were his talents?
- Was there anything in his early childhood that you think could have contributed to him getting involved in crime?

Can you tell me about his late childhood/teenage years?

- What was he like as a teenager?
- How was he different from other teenagers?
- Was he challenging as a teenager? Why?/Why not?
- What were his talents?
- Was there anything in his late childhood / early teenage years that you think could have contributed to him getting involved in crime?

What is your impression of the kind of support R has received from social service agencies over the years?

- Can you remember something specific that seemed helpful to him?
- Did he have a caseworker or probation officer who seemed helpful/supportive?
- Can you think of any type of intervention that could have helped him to stay away from the streets?

As far as you know, can you describe to me how R got involved in crime?

- Why do you think he ended up at Pine Grove?
- If R does not serve a life sentence: What is your prognosis? Do you think R will get in trouble again after he is released?
- In your opinion, how could R be supported most effectively and what would it take to keep him out of prison after he is released?

Have you visited R in Pine Grove?
How do you stay in touch with him?
How regular is your contact with him?
What do you think he gets out of the program?
If you had to use one word to describe R, what would that be?

Notes

INTRODUCTION

1. According to a Pew Research Center survey only 36 percent of Americans believe that the government is doing a good job "helping people get out of poverty" (5). Even among the group making less than $30,000 annually, only 49 percent would prefer a "bigger government and more service" (38). See Pew Research Center, "Beyond Distrust: How Americans View Their Government," November 2015, www.people-press.org/files/2015/11/11-23-2015-Governance-release.pdf (accessed March 6, 2018).

2. The American Presidency Project, "The President's News Conference," August 12, 1986, www.presidency.ucsb.edu/ws/?pid = 37733 (accessed March 6, 2018).

3. The USDA continues to subsidize U.S. agricultural businesses generously. For a list of the current subsidies for agricultural businesses, see www.nal.usda.gov/agricultural-subsidies (accessed March 6, 2018).

4. www.ssa.gov/history/35act.html (accessed March 6, 2018).

5. A detailed accounting of the methodological approach, including interview guides, can be found in the appendices.

6. I do not have access to the young men's juvenile justice files, but their juvenile history tends to come up during PADOC's intake assessment and is regularly mentioned in the files.

1. PUNISHMENT AND THE WELFARE STATE

1. Connecting access to welfare benefits with certain behavioral requirements remains common practice. Residents who have committed a felony, for example, are often denied access to Section 8 housing.

2. For a recent argument against the assumption that a monolithic penal state follows a single logic, see Rubin and Phelps 2017.

3. In *Estelle v. Gamble*, 429 U.S. 97 (1976), the opinion of the Court cited the prevention of cruel and unusual punishment as a mandate to provide health care for prisoners.

4. Between 1992 and 1997 forty-four states passed laws that made it easier to transfer juveniles to the adult criminal justice system (Snyder and Sickmund 1999).

5. See www.nytimes.com/2017/04/10/nyregion/raise-the-age-new-york .html?_r = 0 (accessed April 19, 2017).

6. "Among the offenses that trigger an automatic transfer are murder, involuntary manslaughter, rape, use of a deadly weapon, robbery of a motor vehicle, kidnapping, voluntary manslaughter or aggravated assault."

7. "Title 43 § 6355. Transfer to Criminal Proceedings," www.legis.state.pa.us /cfdocs/legis/LI/consCheck.cfm?txtType = HTM&ttl = 42&div = 0&chpt = 63&sctn = 55&subsctn = 0 (accessed April 19, 2017).

8. www.weeklystandard.com/the-coming-of-the-super-predators/article /8160 (accessed April 19, 2017).

9. See http://old.post-gazette.com/regionstate/20001212pinegroveg5.asp (accessed April 24, 2017).

10. For a detailed look at PREA regulations, see www.prearesourcecenter.org /training-technical-assistance/prea-101/juvenile-facility-standards (accessed April 26, 2017).

11. These are the latest numbers made available on the PADOC website. See www.cor.pa.gov/About%20Us/Statistics/Documents/Budget%20Documents /2011%20Cost%20and%20Population.pdf (accessed April 26, 2017).

12. OJJDP Statistical Briefing Book, December 13, 2015. Available at www .ojjdp.gov/ojstatbb/crime/JAR_Display.asp?ID = qa05201 (accessed May 3, 2017).

13. www.theatlantic.com/politics/archive/2016/07/the-precarious-posi-tion-of-the-new-gop-orthodoxy-on-crime/491735/ (accessed May 3, 2017).

2. THE MAKING OF LIFE-COURSE-PERSISTENT OFFENDERS

1. Despite this staggering level of self-reported trauma, the estimates I provide are likely conservative. Even in retrospective interviews child abuse is substantially underreported, while false positive reporting is considered to be highly unlikely (Hardt and Rutter 2004).

2. The methodological appendix contains a more detailed discussion of the interviews and the specific reasons why the respondents likely felt willing to share sensitive information with me.

3. For information on the RST, see Latessa et al. 2009.

4. This kind of argumentation became well known to broader audiences through the publication of the controversial *The Bell Curve: Intelligence and Class Structure in American Life* (Herrnstein and Murray 1994). For a critique see Fischer et al. (1996).

5. Dewey's work is a precursor to several modern sociological theories that have attempted to unpack the relationship between the individual agent and

social structure. Defined as embodied history Pierre Bourdieu's habitus reso-nates with Dewey's concept of habit. In contrast to Dewey, Bourdieu focuses on the implications habitus has for social mobility. In "Distinction: A Social Critique of the Judgment of Taste," Bourdieu describes habitus as the mecha-nism that binds the individual, their taste, and aspirations to a particular class position. Similar to Dewey's "habit," Bourdieu's habitus represents a form of behavior subconsciously manifesting itself in relation to structure. In contrast to Bourdieu, Dewey is less concerned with social closure.

Describing the formation of habit as a reflection of societal structures and the values attached to them, Dewey focuses explicitly on the responsibility of society for the individual's moral formation. Ann Swidler is another modern social theo-rist whose ideas closely resemble Dewey's theory of habit formation. In "Culture in Action," Swidler (1986) argues that disadvantaged and middle-class children share a similar set of values. She maintains that children growing up in poor neighborhoods do not act according to their actual values because they lack the "cultural tools" to develop adequate strategies for action. This inability to recon-cile opportunities and goals leads to frustration that may be channeled into devi-ant behavior. Swidler develops a concept of culture that is action focused. Similar to Dewey, she implies that given the right tools—for example, educational oppor-tunities—disadvantaged children can develop strategies of action that may allow them to reach their goal without resorting to criminal behavior. I am focusing on Dewey in this book because his work implies the moral obligation of society to ensure the formation of the habits that the collective deems desirable.

3. THE END OF CHILDHOOD

1. PADOC Memo, March 19, 2013, Definition of Young Adult Offender for ACA audits.

2. PADOC also does not require parental consent for research with YAOs under the age of eighteen.

3. Chapter 4 will exclusively focus on the fracture of close family ties.

4. The interviews already reflect the opioid epidemic that has since tight-ened its grip on Pennsylvania. While parents were drawn to crack or alcohol, their children mostly got high on "oxy's" and marijuana.

5. In the NSDUH "illicit drugs" include marijuana, cocaine, heroin, halluci-nogens, and inhalants, as well as the nonmedical use of prescription-type pain relievers, tranquilizers, stimulants, and sedatives.

6. This episode is detailed in chapter 1.

7. It is likely that the head injuries Bryan sustained contributed to his vio-lent behavior (Farrer and Hedges 2011; Moffitt 1993).

4. THE WEAKNESS OF STRONG TIES

1. Social network analysis (SNA) has long been a staple in sociological research (Granovetter 1973). Yet, it has only begun to play a more prominent

role in criminological research during the past decade. Currently, criminologists use SNA to operationalize long-held assumptions about group-level mechanisms such as social control or collective efficacy (Papachristos 2014). With the help of SNA, an individual's criminal behavior can be connected to the specific properties his or her network professes (Young 2011; Kreager 2004; Haynie 2001). SNA has also shown to be useful for predicting patterns of gang homicide (Papachristos 2009) and the nature of heroin-trafficking rings (Natarajan 2006). Most recently, SNA has allowed researchers to gain a better understanding of the prison environment, specifically how status and power are attributed among a group of inmates (Kreager et al. 2016; Kreager et al. 2017). We also know that social ties, especially those that connect former inmates to pro-social, nondeviant family members, aid successful reentry (Agnew 1992; Sampson and Laub 2005; Berg and Huebner 2011).

5. MASCULINITY AND VIOLENCE

1. Tyler shared his story with me because he believes my book and by extension his story is going to help other people.

2. See, for example, www.topix.com/forum/city/downingtown-pa/ TD2A275ATHLN3KVOL/glen-mills-schools (accessed July 12, 2017).

3. See http://ctmirror.org/2012/10/22/sending-children-live-out-state-whose-decision-it/ (accessed June 20, 2016).

4. www.youtube.com/watch?v = Eu3bf7Ma-LQ (accessed July 11, 2017).

5. For more information see Dietmar Sturzbecher, *Potsdamer Beitraege zur Bildungs-, Jugend- und Familienforschung: Glen Mills Schools—Chancen und Grenzen für die Arbeit mit schwierigen Jugendlichen in Deutschland,* December 8, 2004, at ifk-potsdam.de/wp-content/uploads/GMS_Broschüre_Gesamt dokument.pdf (accessed July 21, 2017).

6. See Glen Mills brochure, 2015, at www.glenmillsschool.org/pdfs /GMSBrochure_2015.pdf (accessed July 21, 2017). It is notable that the 2015 brochure does not mention any of the confrontational strategies.

7. www.nytimes.com/1990/01/29/opinion/a-place-for-hard-foster-care-cases .html (accessed July 21, 2017).

6. LOSING CHILDREN

1. See Bureau of Justice Statistics, *Prisoners in 2015,* December 2016, www. bjs.gov/content/pub/pdf/p15_sum.pdf (accessed August 6, 2017).

2. Not being able to provide a working phone number of a relative, for example, signifies not only financial instability, but also an emotional distance between the inmate and his family.

3. Even though I was able to write down her replies almost verbatim, I am not directly quoting her but summarizing her answers.

CONCLUSION AND POLICY IMPLICATIONS

1. For details about SNAP in Pennsylvania see www.dhs.pa.gov/citizens /supplementalnutritionassistanceprogram/ (accessed March 24, 2018). For details about TANF in Pennsylvania see www.dhs.pa.gov/publications/info-graphics/whatisTANF/index.htm and www.compass.state.pa.us/compass.web /menuitems/CashFAQ.aspx?Language = EN (both accessed March 24, 2018).

2. According to census data the median rent in Philadelphia was $949 from 2011–16; see www.census.gov/quickfacts/fact/table/philadelphiacountypenn-sylvania/PST045217 (accessed March 21, 2018).

3. An example of such a limited government welfare program is the Low-Income Home Energy Assistance Program, which helps families to pay for their energy costs; see www.dhs.pa.gov/citizens/heatingassistanceliheap/index.htm (accessed March 24, 2018).

4. The young men's high recidivism rates are in line with previous research. A study by the Bureau of Justice Statistics finds that three years post-release, 67.8 percent of prisoners had recidivated (Durose et al. 2014). Criminologists agree that incarceration temporarily incapacitates people but does not deter them from reof-fending (Nagin, Cullen, and Johnson 2009; Mulvey 2011; Nagin and Snodgrass 2013).

5. For current welfare rates in Germany see www.familien-wegweiser.de /wegweiser/stichwortverzeichnis,did = 47780.html (accessed March 24, 2018).

6. See www.faz.net/aktuell/wirtschaft/wirtschaftspolitik/deutschland-belegt-spitzenplatz-bei-steuern-sozialabgaben-14967504.html (accessed September 29, 2017).

7. It is challenging, and some may argue impossible, to compare a diverse and much larger country like the United States to homogenous and relatively small societies like Sweden, Germany, and the Netherlands that, for the most part, can rely on a common consensus on Judeo-Christian values. I argue that looking to Europe as an example remains useful as long as we keep in mind the different logistical and cultural circumstances of the United States.

8. For more information about this government-sponsored program see Elisabeth Helming, Herbert Blüml, and Heinz Schattner, *Handbuch Sozialpädagogische Familienhilfe—Bundesministerium für Familie, Senioren, Frauen und Jugend*, Schriftenreihe Band 182 (Stuttgart, 1999).

APPENDIX I. METHODOLOGICAL REFLECTIONS

1. Because of IRB stipulation and limited resources I had to exclude those inmates who are under eighteen and would have needed parental consent to participate in the study.

2. One inmate was sent to the restricted housing unit after I conducted the first interview and could not be re-interviewed over the course of the study.

References

Agnew, Robert. 1992. "Foundation for a General Strain Theory of Crime and Delinquency." *Criminology* 30:47–87.

Alexander, Michelle. 2010. *The New Jim Crow*. New York: New Press.

Anderson, Signe Hald, and Christopher Wildeman. 2014. "Paternal Incarceration and Foster Care Placement: The Effect of Paternal Incarceration on Children's Risk of Foster Care Placement." *Social Forces* 93(1): 269–98.

Ary, Dennis V., Terry E. Duncan, Susan C. Duncan, and Hyman Hops. 1999. "Adolescent Problem Behavior: The Influence of Parents and Peers." *Behavior Research and Therapy* 37: 217–30.

Baglivio, Michael T., and Nathan Epps. 2016. "The Interrelatedness of Adverse Childhood Experiences among High-Risk Juvenile Offenders." *Youth Violence and Juvenile Justice* 14(3): 179–98.

Becker, Elizabeth. 2001. "As Ex-Theorist on Young 'Superpredators', Bush Aide Has Regrets." *New York Times*, February 9. Accessed October 3, 2017. www.nytimes.com/2001/02/09/us/as-ex-theorist-on-young-superpredators-bush-aide-has-regrets.html.

Beijrs, Joris, Catrien Bijleveld, Steve van de Weijer, and Aart Liefbroer. 2017. "'All in the Family?': The Relationship between Sibling Offending and Offending Risk." *Journal of Development and Life Course Criminology* 3: 1–14.

Berg, Mark, and Beth M. Huebner. 2011. "Reentry and the Ties That Bind: An Examination of Social Ties, Employment, and Recidivism." *Justice Quarterly* 28(2): 382–410.

Bijleveld, Catrien, and Miriam Wijkman. 2009. "Intergenerational Continuity in Convictions: A Five-Generation Study." *Criminal Behavior and Mental Health* 19: 142–55.

Bishop, Donna M., Charles E. Frazier, Lonn Lanza-Kaduce, and Lawrence Winner. 1996. "The Transfer of Juveniles to Criminal Court: Does It Make a Difference?" *Crime and Delinquency* 42: 171–91.

Blau, Peter M. 1986. *Exchange and Power in Social Life*. Piscataway, NJ: Transaction.

Bourdieu, Pierre. 2001. "Distinction: A Social Critique of the Judgment of Taste." In *The Inequality Reader: Contemporary and Foundational Readings in Race, Class, and Gender*, edited by David B. Grusky and Szonja Szelényi. Boulder, CO: Westview Press.

Bourgois, Philippe. 2002. *In Search of Respect: Selling Crack in El Barrio*. 2nd ed. New York: Cambridge University Press.

Brewster, Karin L., and Irene Padavic. 2002. "No More Kin Care? Change in Black Mothers' Reliance on Relatives for Child Care, 1977–94." *Gender and Society* 16(4): 546–63.

Burawoy, Michael. 1991. "The Extended Case Study Method." In *Ethnography Unbound: Power and Resistance in the Modern Metropolis*, edited by Michael Burawoy, Alice Burton, Ann Arnett Ferguson, and Kathryn J. Fox, 271–87. Berkeley: University of California Press.

Chambliss, William. 1969. *Crime and the Legal Process*. New York: McGraw-Hill.

Chiricos, Theodore G., and Gordon P. Waldo. 1975. "Socioeconomic Status and Criminal Sentencing: An Empirical Assessment of a Conflict Proposition." *American Sociological Review* 40(6): 753–72.

Clear, Todd, and Natasha Frost. 2013. *The Punishment Imperative: The Rise and Failure of Mass Incarceration in America*. New York: New York University Press.

Cohen, Albert Kircidel. 1955. *Delinquent Boys: The Culture of the Gang*. Glencoe, IL: Free Press.

Cohen, Cathy. 2004. "Deviance as Resistance." *Du Bois Review: Social Science Research on Race* 1(1): 27–45.

Comfort, Megan. 2003. "In the Tube at San Quentin: The 'Secondary Prisonization' of Women Visiting Inmates." *Journal of Contemporary Ethnography* 32(1): 77–107.

———. 2008. *Doing Time Together: Love and Family in the Shadow of the Prison*. Chicago: University of Chicago Press.

Contreras, Randol. 2013. *The Stickup Kids: Race, Drugs, Violence, and the American Dream*. Berkeley: University of California Press.

Cunningham, Hugh, and Pier Paolo Viazzo, eds. 1996. *Child Labour in Historical Perspective 1800–1995*. Florence: UNICEF ICDC.

Deitch, Michele, Amanda Barstow, Leslie Lukens, and Ryan Reyna. 2009. *From Time Out to Hard Time: Young Children in the Adult Criminal Justice System*. Austin: University of Texas at Austin, LBJ School of Public Affairs.

Dellafemina, D., C.A. Yeager, and D.O. Lewis. 1990. "Child Abuse: Adolescent Records vs. Adult Recall." *Child Abuse and Neglect* 14(1): 227–31.

Desmond, Matthew. 2012. "Disposable Ties and the Urban Poor." *American Journal of Sociology* 117(5): 1295–335.

———. 2016. *Evicted: Poverty and Profit in the American City*. New York: Crown.

Dewey, John. 1988. *Human Nature and Conduct: The Middle Works of John Dewey 1899–1924*, edited by Ann J. Boydston. Carbondale: Southern Illinois University Press.

Dilulio, John. 1995. "The Coming of the Superpredators." *Weekly Standard,* November 27.

Dominguez, Sylvia, and Celeste Watkins. 2003. "Creating Networks for Survival and Mobility: Social Capital among African-American and Latin-American Low-Income Mothers." *Social Problems* 50(1): 111–35.

Duncan, Greg J., Jean W. Yeung, Jeanne Brooks-Gunn, and Judith R. Smith. 1998. "How Much Does Childhood Affect the Life Chances of Children?" *American Sociological Review* 63(3): 406–23.

Durose, Matthew R., Alexia D. Cooper, and Howard N. Snyder. 2014. *Recidivism of Prisoners Released in 30 States in 2005: Patterns from 2005 to 2010.* Bureau of Justice Statistics Special Report, April, NCJ 244205.

Edin, Kathryn, and Laura Lein. 1997. *Making Ends Meet: How Single Mothers Survive Welfare and Low-Wage Work.* New York: Russell Sage Foundation.

Edin, Kathryn, and Luke H. Shaefer. 2015. *$2 A Day: Living on Almost Nothing in America.* New York: Houghton Mifflin Harcourt.

Epstein, Helen. 1979. *Children of the Holocaust: Conversations with Sons and Daughters of Survivors.* New York: Penguin.

Erikson, Erik H. 1994. *Identity: Youth and Crisis.* New York: W.W. Norton.

Erikson, Kai T. 1996. *Wayward Puritans: A Study in the Sociology of Deviance.* Boston: Allyn & Bacon.

Fagan, Jeffrey. 1996. "The Comparative Advantage of Juvenile Versus Criminal Court Sanctions on Recidivism among Adolescent Felony Offenders." *Law and Policy* 18(1–2): 77–114.

Farrer, Thomas J., and Dawson W. Hedges. 2011. "Prevalence of Traumatic Brain Injury in Incarcerated Groups Compared to the General Population: A Meta-Analysis." *Progress in Neuro-Psychopharmacology and Biological Psychiatry* 35(2): 390–94.

Farrington, David P., Derrick Jolliffe, Rolf Loeber Magda Stouthamer-Loeber, and Larry M. Kalb. 2001. "The Concentration of Offenders in Families, and Family Criminality in the Prediction of Boys' Delinquency." *Journal of Adolescence* 24: 579–96.

Feinberg, Irwin. 1982. "Schizophrenia: Caused by a Fault in Programmed Synaptic Elimination during Adolescence." *Journal of Psychiatric Research* 17(4): 319–34.

Feld, Barry C. 1999. *Bad Kids: Race and the Transformation of the Juvenile Court.* New York: Oxford University Press.

Felitti Vincent J., Robert F. Anda, Dale Nordenberg, et al. 1998. "Relationship of Childhood Abuse and Household Dysfunction to Many of the Leading Causes of Death in Adults: The Adverse Childhood Experiences (ACE) Study." *American Journal of Preventive Medicine* 14(4): 245–58.

Felson, Marcus, and Lawrence E. Cohen. 1979. "Social Change and Crime Rate Trends: A Routine Activity Approach." *American Sociological Review* 44(4): 588–608.

Fergusson, David M., Joseph M. Boden, and John Horwood. 2008. "Exposure to Childhood Sexual and Physical Abuse and Adjustment in Early Adulthood." *Child Abuse and Neglect* 32: 607–19.

Fergusson, David M., Nicole Swain-Campbell, and John Horwood. 2004. "How Does Childhood Disadvantage Lead to Crime?" *Journal of Child Psychology and Psychiatry* 45(5): 956–66.

Fischer, Claude S., et al. 1996. *Inequality by Design: Cracking the Bell Curve Myth*. Princeton, NJ: Princeton University Press.

Foerstner, Jens, and Jens Weidner. 2005. *Internatserziehung fuer kriminelle Jugendliche. Die Glen Mills Schools jetzt in Europa. Vom Entwicklungsstand Holland und Entwicklungsland Deutschland*. Godesberg: Forum Verlag.

Ford, Julian, John Chapman, Daniel F. Connor, and Keith R. Cruise. 2012. "Complex Trauma and Aggression in Secure Juvenile Justice Settings: Criminal Justice and Behavior." *Criminal Justice and Behavior* 39(6): 694–72.

Forrest, Stuart. 2016. *Down and Out and Under Arrest. Policing and Everyday Life in Skid Row*. Chicago: University of Chicago Press.

Foucault, Michel. 1995. *Discipline and Punish: The Birth of the Prison*. New York: Vintage.

Fox-Piven, Francis, and Richard A. Cloward. 1993. *Regulating the Poor: The Function of Public Welfare*. New York: Vintage.

Frazier, Franklin. E. 1939. *The Negro Family in the United States*. South Bend, IN: University of Notre Dame Press.

Garland, David. 2001. *The Culture of Control: Crime and Social Order in Contemporary Society*. Chicago: University of Chicago Press.

Gearan, Anne, and Abby Philip. 2016. "Clinton Regrets 1996 Remarks after Encounter with Activist." *Washington Post*, February 25. Accessed October 3, 2017. www.washingtonpost.com/news/post-politics/wp/2016/02/25/clinton-heckled-by-black-lives-matter-activist/?utm_term = .b8be1cba5347.

Gerstel, Naomi. 2011. "Rethinking Families and Community: The Color, Class, and Centrality of Extended Kin Ties." *Sociological Forum* 26(1): 1–20.

Glaeser, Barney G., and Anselm Strauss. 2009. *The Discovery of Grounded Theory: Strategies for Qualitative Research*. New York: Taylor and Francis.

Glueck, Sheldon, and Eleanor Glueck. 1950. *Unraveling Juvenile Delinquency*. New York: Commonwealth Fund.

Goffman, Alice. 2014. *On the Run: Fugitive Life in an American City*. Chicago: University of Chicago Press.

Gottfredson, Michael R., and Travis Hirschi. 1990. *A General Theory of Crime*. Stanford, CA: Stanford University Press.

Graif, Corina, Andrew S. Gladfelter, and Stephen A. Matthews. 2014. "Urban Poverty and Neighborhood Effects on Crime: Incorporating Spatial and Network Perspectives." *Sociology Compass* 8: 1140–55.

Granovetter, Mark S. 1973. "The Strength of Weak Ties." *American Journal of Sociology* 78(6): 1360–80.

Griffin, Patrick, Sean Addie, Benjamin Adams, and Kathy Firestine. 2011. "Trying Juveniles as Adults: An Analysis of State Transfer Laws and Reporting." Juvenile Offenders and Victims: National Report Series. Washington, DC: Office of Juvenile Justice and Delinquency Prevention.

Grissom, Grant, and William L. Dubnov. 1989. *Without Locks and Bars: Reforming Our Reform Schools*. New York: Praeger.

Groves, Robert M., Floyd J. Fowler, Mick P. Couper, James M. Lepkowski, Eleanor Singer, and Roger Tourangeau. 2004. *Survey Methodology.* Hoboken, NJ: Wiley-Interscience.

Haney, Lynne. 2010. *Offending Women: Power, Punishment, and the Regulation of Desire.* Berkeley: University of California Press.

Harcourt, Bernard. 2013. *Against Prediction: Profiling, Policing and Punishing in an Actuarial Age.* Chicago: University of Chicago Press.

Harding, David J. 2010. *Living the Drama: Community, Conflict, and Culture among Inner-City Boys.* Chicago: University of Chicago Press.

Hardt, Jochen, and Michael Rutter. 2004. "Validity of Adult Retrospective Reports of Adverse Childhood Experiences: Review of the Evidence." *Journal of Child Psychology and Psychiatry* 45(2): 260–73.

Haynie, Dana L. 2001. "Delinquent Peers Revisited: Does Network Structure Matter?" *American Journal of Sociology* 106(4):1013–57.

Heide, Kathleen M., and Eldra P. Solomon. 2006. "Biology, Childhood Trauma and Murder: Rethinking Justice." *International Journal of Law and Psychiatry* 29: 220–33.

Herrnstein, Richard J., and Charles Murray. 1994. *The Bell Curve: Intelligence and Class Structure in American Life.* New York: Free Press.

Jensen, Eric, and Linda K. Metsger. 1994. "A Test of the Deterrent Effect of Legislative Waiver on Violent Juvenile Crime." *Crime and Delinquency* 40(1): 96–104.

Jerolmack, Colin, and Shamus Khan. 2014. "Talk Is Cheap: Ethnography and the Attitudinal Fallacy." *Sociological Methods and Research* 43(2): 178–209.

Jiang, Yang, Maribel R. Granja, and Heather Koball. 2017. "Basic Facts about Low-Income Children: Children under 3 Years, 2015." National Center for Children in Poverty, Columbia University Mailman School of Public Health.

Katz, Jack. 1988. *Seductions of Crime: Moral and Sensual Attractions in Doing Evil.* New York: Basic Books.

Khan, Shamus Rahman. 2011. *Privilege: The Making of an Adolescent Elite at St. Paul's School.* Princeton, NJ: Princeton University Press.

King, Nicholas B., Veronique Fraser, Constantina Boikos, Robin Richardson, and Sam Harper. 2014. "Determinants of Increased Opioid-Related Mortality in the United States and Canada, 1990–2013: A Systematic Review." *American Journal of Public Health* 104(8): 32–42.

Koenen, Karestan C., Terrie E. Moffitt, Richie Poulton, and Judith Martin. 2007. "Early Childhood Factors Associated with the Development of Post-Traumatic Stress Disorder: Results from a Longitudinal Birth Cohort." *Psychological Medicine* 37(2): 181–92.

Kreager, Derek A. 2004. "Strangers in the Halls: Isolation and Delinquency in School Networks." *Social Forces* 83(1): 351–90.

Kreager, Derek A., David R. Schaefer, Martin Bouchard, Dana L. Haynie, Sara Wakefield, Jacob Young, and Gary Zajac. 2016. "Toward a Criminology of Inmate Networks." *Justice Quarterly* 33(6): 1000–1028.

Kreager, Derek, Jacob T. N. Young, Dana L. Haynie, Martin Bouchard, David R. Schaefer, and Gary Zajac. 2017. "Where 'Old Heads' Prevail: Inmate Hierarchy in a Men's Prison Unit." *American Sociological Review* 82(4): 685–718.

Kupchik, Aaron. 2006. *Judging Juveniles: Prosecuting Adolescents in Adult and Juvenile Courts.* New York: NYU Press.

———. 2016. *The Real School Safety Problem: The Long-Term Consequences of Harsh School Punishment.* Berkeley: University of California Press.

Lahey, Jessica. 2016. "The Steep Costs of Keeping Juveniles in Adult Prison." *The Atlantic*, January 8. Accessed October 3, 2017. www.theatlantic.com/education /archive/2016/01/the-cost-of-keeping-juveniles-in-adult-prisons/423201/.

Lareau, Annette. 2003. *Unequal Childhoods: Class, Race, and Family Life.* Berkeley: University of California Press.

Latessa, Edward J., Paula Smith, Myrinda Schweitzer, and Lori Lovins. 2009. *Evaluation of Selected Institutional Offender Treatment Programs for the Pennsylvania Department of Corrections.* Washington, DC: Justice Research and Statistics Association.

Laub, John H., and Robert J. Sampson. 2003. *Shared Beginnings, Divergent Lives: Delinquent Boys to Age 70.* Cambridge, MA: Harvard University Press.

LeBel, Thomas P., Ros Burnett, Shadd Maruna, and Shawn Bushway. 2008. "The 'Chicken and Egg' of Subjective and Social Factors in Desistance from Crime." *European Journal of Criminology* 5(2): 131–59.

Lee, Rosalyn, Xiangming Fang, and Feijun Luo. 2013. "The Impact of Parental Incarceration on the Physical and Mental Health of Young Adults." *Pediatrics* 131: 1188–95.

Levine, Judith. 2013. *Ain't No Trust: How Bosses, Boyfriends, and Bureaucrats Fail Low-Income Mothers and Why It Matters.* Berkeley: University of California Press.

Lewis, Oscar. 1975. *Five Families: Mexican Case Studies in the Culture of Poverty.* New York: Basic Books.

Listenbee, Robert, Joe Torre, et al. 2012. *Report of the Attorney General's National Task Force on Children Exposed to Violence,* December 12. Office of Juvenile Justice and Delinquency Prevention, Office of Justice Programs, U.S. Department of Justice. Accessed October 3, 2017. www.justice.gov /defendingchildhood/cev-rpt-full.pdf.

Loeber, Rolf, and Magda Stouthamer-Loeber. 1986. "Family Factors as Correlates and Predictors of Juvenile Conduct Problems and Delinquency." *Crime and Justice: A Review of Research* 7: 29–149.

Lopoo, Leonard M., and Bruce Western. 2005. "Incarceration and the Formation and Stability of Marital Unions." *Journal of Marriage and Family* 67(3): 721–34.

Mack, Julian. 1909. "The Juvenile Court." *Harvard Law Review* 23(2): 104–22.

Martinson, Robert. 1974. "What Works? Questions and Answers about Prison Reform." *Public Interest* 35: 22–54.

Massey, Douglas, and Nancy Denton. 1993. *American Apartheid: Segregation and the Making of the Underclass.* Cambridge, MA: Harvard University Press.

Massoglia, Michael. 2008. "Incarceration, Health, and Racial Disparities in Health." *Law and Society Review* 42: 275–306.

Masten, Ann S. 2001. "Ordinary Magic: Resilience Processes in Development." *American Psychologist* 56(3): 227–38.

———— and Douglas J. Coatsworth. 1998. "The Development of Competence in Favorable and Unfavorable Environments: Lessons from Research on Successful Children." *American Psychologist* 53(2): 205–20.

MacLeod, Jay. 2008. *Ain't No Makin' It: Aspirations and Attainment in a Low-Income Neighborhood.* Boulder, CO: Westview Press.

Mead, George Herbert. 1918. "The Psychology of Punitive Justice." *American Journal of Sociology* 23(5): 577–602.

Merton, Robert K. 1938. "Social Structure and Anomie." *American Sociological Review* 3(5): 672–82.

Messerschmidt, James. 1993. *Masculinities and Crime: Critique and Reconceptualization of Theory.* Lanham, MD: Rowman and Littlefield.

Mill, John Stuart. [1869] 1978. *On Liberty.* Edited by Elizabeth Rappaport. Indianapolis and Cambridge: Hackett.

Miller-Cribbs, Julie, and Naomi Farber. 2008. "Kin Networks and Poverty among African Americans: Past and Present." *Social Work* 53: 43–51.

Moffitt, Robert. 2008. "A Primer on U.S. Welfare Reform." *Focus* 26(1): 15–25.

Moffitt, Terrie E. 1993. "Adolescence-Limited and Life-Course-Persistent Antisocial Behavior: A Developmental Taxonomy." *Psychological Review* 100(4): 674–701.

Moynihan, Daniel P. 1965. *The Negro Family: The Case for National Action.* Office of Policy Planning and Research, United States Department of Labor.

Mulvey, Edward P. 2011. *Highlights from Pathways to Desistance: A Longitudinal Study of Serious Adolescent Offenders.* Office of Juvenile Justice and Delinquency Prevention, Juvenile Justice Fact Sheet (March). Accessed October 3, 2017. www.ncjrs.gov/pdffiles1/ojjdp/230971.pdf.

Nagin, Daniel S., Francis T. Cullen, and Cheryl Lero Johnson. 2009. "Imprisonment and Reoffending." In *Crime and Justice: A Review of Research,* vol. 38, edited by Michael Tonry, 115–200. Chicago: University of Chicago Press Journals.

Nagin, Daniel S., and Matthew Snodgrass. 2013. "The Effect of Incarceration on Re-Offending: Evidence from a Natural Experiment in Pennsylvania." *Journal of Quantitative Criminology* 26: 601–42.

Natarajan, Mangai. 2006. "Understanding the Structure of a Large Heroin Distribution Network: A Quantitative Analysis of Qualitative Data." *Journal of Quantitative Criminology* 22: 171–92.

Nelson, Margaret. 2000. "Single Mothers and Social Support: The Commitment to, and Retreat from, Reciprocity." *Qualitative Sociology* 23: 291–317.

Pager, Devah. 2003. "The Mark of a Criminal Record." *American Journal of Sociology* 108(5): 937–75.

Papachristos, Andrew V. 2009. "Murder by Structure: Dominance Relations and the Social Structure of Gang Homicide." *American Journal of Sociology* 115(1): 74–128.

———. 2014. "The Network Structure of Crime." *Sociology Compass* 8(4): 347–57.

Patterson, Orlando. 1998. *Rituals of Blood: Consequences of Slavery in Two American Centuries.* Washington, DC: Civitas.

Pattillo-McCoy, Mary. 1999. *Black Picket Fences: Privilege and Peril among the Black Middle Class.* Chicago: University of Chicago Press.

Phelps, Michelle. 2011. "Rehabilitation in the Punitive Era: The Gap between Rhetoric and Reality in U.S. Prison Programs." *Law and Society Review* 45(1): 33–68.

Platt, Alexander M. 1977. *The Child Savers: The Invention of Delinquency.* 2nd ed. Chicago: University of Chicago Press.

Putman, Robert D. 2001. *Bowling Alone: The Collapse and Revival of American Community.* New York: Touchstone Books.

Raudenbush, Danielle. 2016. "'I Stay by Myself': Social Support, Distrust, and Selective Solidarity among the Urban Poor." *Sociological Forum* 31(4): 1018–39.

Reich, Adam. 2010. *Hidden Truth: Young Men Navigating Lives in and out of Juvenile Prison.* Berkeley: University of California Press.

Rhodes, Lorna A. 2004. *Total Confinement: Madness and Reason in the Maximum Security Prison.* Berkeley: University of California Press.

Rios, Victor M. 2011. *Punished: Policing the Lives of Black and Latino Boys.* New York: NYU Press.

Rodriguez, Nancy. 2016. "Bridging the Gap between Research and Practice: The Role of Science in Addressing the Effects of Incarceration on Family Life." *Annals of the American Academy of Political and Social Science* 651: 231–40.

Roettger, Michael E., and Jason D. Boardman D. 2012. "Parental Incarceration and Gender-Based Risks for Increased Body Mass Index: Evidence from the National Longitudinal Study of Adolescent Health in the United States." *American Journal of Epidemiology* 175(7): 636–44.

Roschelle, Anne. 1997. *No More Kin: Exploring Race, Class, and Gender in Family Networks.* Thousand Oaks, CA: Sage.

Rose, Alex. 2014. "Ex-Teacher Sues Glen Mills over Firing." *Delaware County Daily Times*, November 2. Accessed July 12, 2017. www.delcotimes.com /article/DC/20140211/NEWS/140219919.

Rothman, David J. 1971. *The Discovery of the Asylum: Social Order and Disorder in the New Republic.* New Brunswick, NJ: Transaction.

Rowe, David, and David P. Farrington. 1997. "The Familial Transmission of Criminal Convictions." *Criminology* 35(1): 177–201.

Rubin, Ashley, and Michelle Phelps. 2017. "Fracturing the Penal State: State Actors and the Role of Conflict in Penal Change." *Theoretical Criminology* 21(4): 422–40.

Sampson, Robert J., and Corina Graif. 2009. "Neighborhood Social Capital and Differential Social Organization: Resident and Leadership Dimensions." *American Behavioral Scientist* 52(11): 1579–605.

Sampson, Robert J., and John H. Laub. 2005. "A Life-Course View of the Development of Crime." *Annals of the American Academy of Political and Social Science* 602: 12–45.

Sarkisian, Natalia, and Naomi Gerstel. 2004. "Kin Support among Blacks and Whites: Race and Family Organization." *American Sociological Review* 69: 812–37.

Sekwar, Aswin, Allison R. Bialas, Heather de Rivera, et al. 2016. "Schizophrenia Risk from Complex Variation of Complement Component 4." *Nature* 530: 177–83.

Selemon, Lynn D. 2013. "A Role for Synaptic Plasticity in the Adolescent Development of Executive Function." *Translational Psychiatry* 3(3): e238.

Sharkey, Patrick, Max Besbris, and Michael Friedson. 2016. "Poverty and Crime." In *The Oxford Handbook of the Social Science of Poverty,* edited by David Brady and Linda M. Burton. Accessed March 24, 2018. Oxford Handbooks Online, 10.1093/oxfordhb/9780199914050.013.28.

Shedd, Carla. 2015. *Unequal City: Race, Schools and Perceptions of Injustice.* New York: Russell Sage.

Shonkoff, Jack P., Andrew S. Garner, et al. 2012. "The Lifelong Effects of Early Childhood Adversity and Toxic Stress." *Pediatrics* 129(1): 2011–63.

Soss, Joe, Richard C. Fording, and Sanford F. Schram. 2011. *Disciplining the Poor: Neoliberal Paternalism and the Persistent Power of Race.* Chicago: University of Chicago Press.

Soyer, Michaela. 2014. "'We knew our time had come': The Dynamics of Threat and Microsocial Ties in Three Polish Ghettos under Nazi Oppression." *Mobilization* (19)1: 47–66.

———. 2016. *A Dream Denied: Incarceration, Recidivism and Young Minority Men.* Berkeley: University of California Press.

———, Susan McNeeley, Gary Zajac, and Kristofer Bucklen. 2017. "Measuring the Criminal Mind: The Relationship between Intelligence and CSS-M Results among a Sample of Pennsylvania Prison Inmates." *Criminal Justice and Behavior* 44(11): 1444–61.

Spatz Widom, Cathy. 1989. "The Cycle of Violence." *Science* 244(4901): 160–66.

Stack, Carol B. 1974. *All Our Kin.* New York: Basic Books.

Stolenzberg, Liza, and Stewart J. D'Alessio. 1994. "Sentencing and Unwarranted Disparity: An Empirical Assessment of the Long-Term Impact of Sentencing Guidelines in Minnesota." *Criminology.* 32(2): 301–10.

Strauss, Anselm L., and Barney Glaser. 2009. *The Discovery of Grounded Theory.* Rutgers, NJ: Transaction.

Substance Abuse and Mental Health Services Administration. 2014. *Results from the 2013 National Survey on Drug Use and Health: Summary of National Findings*. NSDUH Series H-48, HHS Publication No. (SMA) 14–4863, Rockville, MD.

Sufrin, Carolyn. 2017. *Jailcare: Finding the Safety Net for Women behind Bars.* Oakland: University of California Press.

Swidler, Ann. 1986. "Culture in Action: Symbols and Strategies." *American Sociological Review* 51(2): 273–86.

Sykes, Gresham M., and David Matza. 1957. "Techniques of Neutralization: A Theory of Delinquency." *American Sociological Review* 22(6): 664–70.

Teplin, Linda A., Karen M. Abram, Gary M. McClelland Gary, Mina K. Dulcan, and Amy A. Mericle. 2002. "Psychiatric Disorders in Youth in Juvenile Detention." *Archives of General Psychiatry* 59: 1133–43.

Terr, Lenore C. 1991. "Childhood Traumas: An Outline and Overview." *American Journal of Psychiatry* 148(1): 11–20.

Thornberry, Terence P. 1973. "Race, Socioeconomic Status and Sentencing in the Juvenile Justice System." *Journal of Criminal Law and Criminology* 64(1): 90–98.

Toner, Robert. 1995. "The 104th Congress: Welfare; Senate Approves Welfare Plan That Would End Aid Guarantee." *New York Times,* September 20. Accessed September 22, 2017. www.nytimes.com/1995/09/20/us/104th-congress-welfare-senate-approves-welfare-plan-that-would-end-aid-guarantee.html?pagewanted = all,%20accessed%20April%2017th%202017.

Turner, Heather A., David Finkelhor, and Richard Ormrod. 2005. "The Effect of Lifetime Victimization on the Mental Health of Children and Adolescents." *Social Science and Medicine* 62: 13–27.

Turner, Nicholas, and Jeremy Travis. 2015. "What We Learned from German Prisons." *New York Times*, August 6. Accessed December 12, 2015. www.nytimes.com/2015/08/07/opinion/what-we-learned-from-german-prisons.html?_r = 0.

Vance, J.D. 2016. *Hillbilly Elegy: A Memoir of a Family and Culture in Crisis.* New York: HarperCollins.

Van Cleve, Nicole Gonzalez. 2016. *Crook County: Racism and Injustice in America's Largest Criminal Court.* Stanford, CA: Stanford University Press.

Vanderbilt-Adriance, Ella, and Daniel S. Shaw. 2008. "Protective Factors and the Development of Resilience in the Context of Neighborhood Disadvantage." *Journal of Abnormal Child Psychology* 36(6): 887–901.

Venkatesh, Sudhir Alladi. 2002. *American Project: The Rise and Fall of a Modern Ghetto.* Cambridge MA: Harvard University Press.

Wacquant, Loïc. 2006. *Body & Soul: Notebooks of an Apprentice Boxer.* New York: Oxford University Press.

———. 2008a. *Urban Outcasts: A Comparative Sociology of Advanced Marginality.* Cambridge: Polity.

———. 2008b. "The Place of the Prison in the New Government of Poverty." In *After the War on Crime: Race, Democracy, and a New Reconstruction,* edited by Mary Frampton et al., 23–36. New York: New York University Press.

―――. 2009. *Punishing the Poor: The Neoliberal Governmentality of Social Inequality*. Durham, NC: Duke University Press.

――― and William Julius Wilson. 1989. "The Cost of Racial and Class Exclusion in the Inner City." *Annals of the American Academy of Political and Social Science* 501(1): 8–25.

Wakefield, Sara, and Christopher Wildeman. 2013. *Children of the Prison Boom: Mass Incarceration and the Future of American Inequality*. New York: Oxford University Press.

Wakefield, Sara, Hedwig Lee, and Christopher Wildeman. 2016. "Tough on Crime, Tough on Families? Criminal Justice and Family Life in America." *Annals of the American Academy of Political and Social Science* 651: 8–21.

Watt, Michael J., Matthew A. Weber, Davies R. Shaydel, and Gina L. Foster. 2017. "Impact of Juvenile Chronic Stress on Adult Cortico-Accumbal Function: Implications for Cognition and Addiction." *Progress in Neuro-Psychopharmacology and Biological Psychiatry* 79(Part B): 136–54.

Weber, Max. 1949. *Max Weber on the Methodology of the Social Sciences*. Edited and translated by Edward A. Shils and Henry A. Finch. Glencoe, IL: Free Press.

―――. 1958. *From Max Weber: Essays in Sociology*. Edited and Translated by Hans H. Gerth and Wright Mills. New York: Oxford University Press.

―――. [1904–5] 2002. *The Protestant Ethic and the "Spirit" of Capitalism and Other Writings*. Edited and translated by Peter Baehr and Gordon C. Wells. New York and London: Penguin Books.

West, Candace, and Don H. Zimmerman. 1987. "Doing Gender." *Gender and Society* 1(2): 125–51.

Western, Bruce. 2006. *Punishment and Inequality in America*. New York: Russell Sage Foundation.

―――, Anthony Braga, Jaclyn Davis, and Catherine Sirois. 2015. "Stress and Hardship after Prison." *American Journal of Sociology* 120(5): 1512–47.

Wildeman, Christopher. 2016. "Parental Incarceration, Child Homelessness, and the Invisible Consequences of Mass Imprisonment." *Annals of the American Academy of Political and Social Science* 651: 74–96.

―――, Jason Schnittker, and Kristin Turney. 2012. "Despair by Association? The Mental Health of Mothers with Children by Recently Incarcerated Fathers." *American Sociological Review* 77(2): 216–43.

Willis, Paul. 1981. *Learning to Labor: How Working Class Kids Get Working Class Jobs*. New York: Columbia University Press.

Wilson, William Julius. 1990. *The Truly Disadvantaged: The Inner City, the Underclass, and Public Policy*. Chicago: University of Chicago Press.

―――. 2009. *More Than Just Race: Being Black and Poor in the Inner City*. New York: W.W. Norton.

Wood, Joanne N., Heather M. Griffis, Christine M. Taylor, Douglas Strane, Gerlinde C. Harb, Lanyu Mi, Lihai Song, Kevin G. Lynch, and David M.

Rubin. 2016. "Under-ascertainment from Healthcare Settings of Child Abuse Events among Children of Soldiers by the U.S. Army Family Advocacy Program." *Child Abuse and Neglect* 63: 202–10.

Yehuda, Rachel, Linda M. Bierer, James Schmeidler, Daniel H. Aferiat, Ilana Breslau, and Susan Dolan. 2001. "Low Cortisol and Risk for PTSD in Adult Offspring of Holocaust Survivors." *American Journal of Psychiatry* 157(8): 1252–59.

Young, Alford A. 2004. *The Minds of Marginalized Black Men: Making Sense of Mobility, Opportunity, and Future Life Chances.* Princeton, NJ: Princeton University Press.

Young, Jacob T.N. 2011. "'How Do They "End Up Together"'? A Social Network Analysis of Self-Control, Homophily, and Adolescent Relationships." *Journal of Quantitative Criminology* 27: 251–73.

Zane, Steven N., Welsh Brandon, and Daniel P. Mears. 2016a. "Juvenile Transfer and the Specific Deterrence Hypothesis: Systematic Review and Meta Analysis." *Criminology and Public Policy* 15(3): 901–25.

Zane, Steven N., Welsh Bradon, and Kevin Drakulich. 2016b. "Assessing the Impact of Race on the Juvenile Waiver Decision: A Systematic Review and Meta Analysis." *Journal of Criminal Justice* 46: 107–16.

Zimring, Franklin E. 2005. *American Juvenile Justice.* Oxford: Oxford University Press.

Index

Abuse, 22, 28, 35, 46, 52, 67, 72–75,
    77–78, 81, 86, 107, 110
  child abuse, 10, 28, 67, 126, 132, 133,
    142
  domestic, 67
  emotional, 9, 23, 31, 49, 75, 79, 81
  physical, 23–26, 67, 72–73, 79–81, 133
  sexual, 23
  verbal, 23–26, 38,
"Act 33", 1, 17, 18, 37
Adolescence, 22, 27, 52–53, 84–85, 117,
    119, 133
Adolescent(s), 20, 53, 121, 131–133
Aid for Families with Dependent Chil-
    dren (AFDC), 12, 66
Agency, 33–34, 36, 81, 100
Agnew, Robert, 2, 9, 36, 128, 131
Aggravated Assault, 6–7, 48–49,
    68, 126
Alcohol abuse, 38, 49
Anomie theory, 1, 137
American Dream, 99, 132
Autonomy, 8, 40, 44, 81, 98

Blau, Peter, 55, 58, 131
Bourdieu, Pierre, 10, 71, 127, 132

Capitalism, 14, 104, 141
  hypercapitalism, 104
Caregiver(s), vii, 9, 23–26, 35, 38–39,
    44, 51–52, 55–57, 63, 65, 85–86,
    94–99, 106, 108

Case Summary File(s), 5, 28, 43, 67,
    68, 108, 110, 122
Caseworker, 73, 74, 121
Child Saving Movement, 16
Clinton, Bill, 12
Clinton, Hillary, 20, 134
Cognitive abilities, 4
  capacity, 37
  deficits, 2
  development, 22, 87
  disadvantage, 27
  maturation, 102
Culture, 2, 71, 76, 111, 127, 132,
    134–136, 140
  of poverty, 2, 50, 54
Cultural capital, 10
Cultural tools, 127
Collective efficacy, 2, 128
Control theory, 2
Crack (drug), 8–9, 38–42, 44, 47,
    50–51, 70, 72, 127, 132
  crack addict, 28, 42
  "crack babies," 51
  crack epidemic, 41, 51
  crack era, 41
  crackhead(s), 48, 72
  smoking, 41, 48, 73,
Crime(s), 1–2,4–5,9, 12, 14, 18, 20,
    33–34, 36, 38, 39, 43, 46–48, 53, 56,
    58–60, 62, 65–66, 69–71, 80, 82,
    84–85, 90, 97, 108–109, 113–114,
    116, 119–121, 123, 126, 131–141

Crime *(continued)*
  aging out of, 27
  pathways into, 32, 39, 53, 58
  juvenile, 20, 99
  prevention of, 20
  violent, 1, 18, 46, 55
Criminal behavior, 1–2,4, 8–11, 23, 33,
    35–36, 46–47, 50–51, 53, 56–57,
    66, 71, 83, 90–91, 95, 97–98,
    127,128, 131

Death, 23–26, 30–31, 42–43, 57, 63–65,
    73, 87, 133
Delinquency, 20, 56, 133, 131, 133–
    138, 140
  delinquent, 56, 75, 132, 135, 136
  juvenile, 56, 66, 134,
Department of Children and Families
    (DCF), 23, 24–26
Depression, 22, 83, 85, 117
Desistance, 82, 136, 137
Deviance, 2, 27, 50, 132–133
Dewey, John, 1,3, 32, 33, 34, 36, 56,
    126, 127, 132
Discipline, vii, 11, 61, 75, 77, 80–81, 90,
    106, 108, 134
  self-discipline, 76
Disadvantage, 1–4, 8, 10–11, 15, 27–28,
    35–36, 40, 49–50, 52–54, 57, 70,
    80, 82, 102, 104, 127, 134, 140, 141
Drugs, 1, 29, 38, 51, 60, 87, 92, 97, 127,
    132
  abuse, 31, 38–39, 50, 56, 140
  addiction, 8, 10, 31, 37–40, 47,
    50–51, 57, 62, 66, 85, 92, 98, 1116,
    119
  dealing, 42, 69
  selling, 34, 42, 44–47, 70–71, 81

Earned Income Tax Credit (EIC), 13,
    14
Economy, 11, 14, 20, 36, 104
  capital 10,27, 38, 105
  hardship, 3, 39, 57, 85, 104
  pressure, 10, 14,47
  resources, 38, 49
Eviction, 1, 59, 132

Felony, 17, 125, 133
Food, 10, 20, 27, 29, 34, 36, 40, 43, 45,
    86–87, 97–98
  insecurity, 10, 52, 55, 57
  service job, 69
  scarcity, 23–26, 38
Food Stamps (SNAP) 13, 45, 74, 98,
    102, 129
Foster care, 3, 29, 31, 41, 45–46, 65,
    73–74, 81, 85, 88, 92 98, 103, 131
Foucault, Michel, 81, 134

Gang(s), 23, 31, 48–50, 94, 116, 119,
    120, 128, 132, 138
Garland, David, 3, 12, 14, 134
Germany, 76, 99, 102–103, 109, 110–
    111, 129
Glen Mills Schools, 9, 67, 75–81, 128,
    134, 138
Glueck, Sheldon and Eleanor, 56, 134
Great Depression, 3
"Great Society," 3
Gun(s), 1, 23, 30, 42, 46, 59, 73, 89, 97

Habitus, 71, 92, 127
Harrisburg, 5, 63, 65
Heroin, 38–39, 62, 70, 127–28, 137
Housing, 13, 18–19, 44, 89, 92, 102,
    125
  insecurity, 10, 24–26, 38, 52–53, 55,
    57
  instability, 66, 89
  project, 55

Identity, 7, 32–33, 68–69, 71, 80–81,
    87, 133
Incarceration, 5, 8–9, 12, 14–15, 20,
    23–26, 81, 83–86, 88, 91–92,
    94–97,99–100, 104, 120, 129, 131–
    132, 136–139, 141
  mass, 10, 12, 14, 50, 84, 99, 132, 141
Income, 60, 92, 104
  gross, 102
  low, 54–55, 129, 133, 135–137
  median, 100
Inequality, 1, 51, 103, 132, 134, 141
In Re Gault, 16

Institutional Review Board (IRB), 105, 129
IQ, 28, 64, 71

Jail(s), 15, 20, 31, 42, 45, 62, 67, 85, 100–101,
Judicial waiver(s), 17
Justice System
  criminal, 1, 2, 3, 8, 9, 10–12, 14, 16–17, 35, 53, 56, 74, 81, 84–85, 94–95, 99, 102, 104, 107, 126, 132
  juvenile, 4, 8, 9, 13, 15–16, 27, 35, 51, 67, 71–72, 74–75, 96, 102, 112, 120–1, 140
Juvenile offender, 18, 110, 131, 134

Kennedy, Edward, 12
Kinship, 66
  ties, 9, 52–54, 66
  network(s), 54, 58, 98

Laub, John, 128, 136, 139
"legislative child abuse," 10
Life-course, 5, 8–9, 12, 82, 84, 108–109, 137, 139
  histories, 34, 36, 94, 106
  interview(s), 106, 112
Low-income, 54–55, 129, 133, 135–137

Martinson, Robert, 14, 136
Masculinity, 9, 67, 71–72, 76
  outsider, 9, 80
Mead, George Herbert, 16, 137
Mental Health, 11, 58, 85, 131, 136, 140–141
  issues, 57, 88
  problems, 22, 27, 52, 57, 87, 88
  needs, 96–97
  services, 8, 19, 35
  support, 22
Merton, Robert, 2, 137
Mill, John Stuart, 33
Mobility, 133, 142
  social, 65, 127
Moffitt Terrie, 2, 127, 135, 137
  life-course-persistent offenders, 8, 22, 27–28, 35, 126, 137,

adolescence-limited offenders, 8, 27, 37, 40, 137
  maturity gap, 8, 27, 37–38, 40, 43, 51,
  reverse maturity gap, 8, 37, 43, 51, 56–57, 98
Moynihan, Patrick, 12
Murder, 1, 6, 15, 30, 41, 48, 87, 126, 135, 138

Narrative(s), 2, 5, 12, 23, 27–28, 32, 40, 43, 50–51, 57, 59, 65, 67,69, 71, 83, 94, 97–98, 107–108
Netherlands, 102, 129
Network(s), 53–55, 66, 85, 99, 108, 128, 133–135, 137–138, 142
  familial, 55–56
  kin(ship), 53–55, 57–58, 65–66, 98
  peer, 2, 32,
  social, 54, 56, 63, 66, 98
Neuropsychology, 27, 32, 133, 141
New Deal, 12

Overdose, 29, 57, 62

Parole, 15–16, 20, 43, 68, 93, 100
Pennsylvania, 1, 5, 17, 18, 60, 67, 75, 76,83, 94, 98, 99, 100, 106, 107, 112, 127, 129
  Pennsylvania Department of Corrections (PADOC), 5, 19, 28, 37, 67, 105, 110, 125, 126, 127, 136, 137, 139
  Pennsylvania State University (Penn State), vii, 99, 105, 106
Personal Responsibility and Work Opportunity Reconciliation Act (PRWORA), 12
Philadelphia, 5, 29, 49, 59, 60, 62, 73, 75, 83, 93, 94, 98, 129
Philadelphia Housing Authority, 98
Pittsburgh, 5, 30, 31, 33, 43, 69, 83
Police, 1, 5, 29, 42, 52, 74
Poverty, 2–4, 9–11, 13–14, 20, 22–26, 28–29, 32, 34–38, 40, 49–57, 60, 65–66, 97–98, 102–104, 125, 132, 134–137, 139

Prison(s) 1, 10–11, 14–16, 18–20, 44, 50, 63–64, 66–67, 72, 74, 83–85, 88, 91, 93–96, 99–102, 105–106, 108– 10, 123, 128, 134, 136, 138– 41

Prison Rape Elimination ACT (PREA), 19, 126

prisonization, secondary, 85, 91, 95,

Privilege, 51, 111, 135, 138

Probation, 20, 43, 68, 71, 79, 80
    officer, 43, 120, 123

Prosecutorial discretion, 17

Public Policy, 51, 103, 141–142

Public Housing, 98

Punishment, 2, 11, 14, 16, 20, 61, 67, 79, 81, 86, 90, 96, 102, 126, 132, 135, 136, 141
    justice, 33, 137
    punitive, 2, 14–15, 20, 74, 138

Race, 6, 19, 24–25, 37, 55, 101, 107, 111, 132–133, 136, 138–142
    mixed, 61, 76, 89

Reagan, Ronald, 3

Recidivism, 14, 18–19, 28, 91, 94–95, 100, 129, 131, 133, 139

Reentry, 16, 84, 94, 128, 131

Rehabilitation 14–16, 37, 81, 102, 138

Restricted Housing Unit 5, 129

Risk measures, 5
    Pennsylvania Risk Screening Tool (RST), 28

Roosevelt, Franklin D, 3

Sampson, Robert, 54, 128, 136, 139,

SCI Pine Grove, vii, 1, 4, 5, 6, 8, 11,12, 15, 16, 18, 83, 84, 88, 91, 92, 94, 99, 100, 105, 106, 107

School(s), 2, 20, 31, 42–51, 59–61, 63, 65, 69–71, 73, 75,-78, 80, 81, 89–93, 110–111, 113, 115, 117– 118, 121–122, 132, 134–136, 139

"School to prison pipeline," 50

"Section 8", 98, 125

Segregation, segregated, 13–14, 40, 54, 66, 92, 109, 137,

Selective Solidarity, 55, 138

Self-control, 2, 15, 142

Self-esteem, 4, 20, 36, 94

Social capital, 27, 49, 61, 105, 133, 139

Social control, 128

Social network(s), 54–56, 63, 66, 98
    Social Network Analysis (SNA), 127, 142

Social ties, 23, 38, 49, 56, 128, 131

Social welfare
    dismantled, 36,96
    needs, 3
    system, 66, 96–97, 99, 103–104

Social worker, 27, 65, 74, 86, 103, 117, 121

Socioeconomic status, 2, 10, 11, 55, 65, 80, 94, 132, 140

Spatz Widom, Cathy, 22, 139

Stack, Carol, 53–55, 65–66, 139

State College, 107

Statutory exclusion, 17

Structure(s)
    class, 126
    family, 54,66
    constitutional, 71
    political, 102
    social, 33, 36, 127, 137, 138

Supervision, 9, 15, 47, 56, 66, 98, 100

Sweden, 102, 129

Super-predators, 12, 15, 20, 32, 126

Synapses, 22

Teacher(s), 30, 45–47, 73–75, 87, 89, 91, 117, 122, 138

Temporary Assistance for Needy Families (TANF), 12, 13, 20, 98, 102, 103, 129

Terr, Lenore, 8, 23, 56, 140,

Theft, 6

Therapist, 27, 47, 59, 65, 117

Trauma 4, 8, 22–23, 27, 32, 34–36, 38, 51–52, 57, 67, 97, 126, 134
    Post Traumatic Stress Disorder (PTSD), 59, 135

Trauma, childhood, 4, 8, 10, 22, 24–27, 32, 34–36, 38–39, 51, 66, 98, 135, 140

traumatic experiences, events, 3–4,
8–9, 22–23, 27–28, 32, 37, 48, 52,
56–57, 64,67, 86, 97–98

Urban areas, 5, 29
decay in, 89
poor, 64, 132, 189
neighborhoods, 34
outcasts, 140
compared to suburbs, 31, 87

Violence, 1, 8–9, 18, 23–24, 28, 30–31,
34–38, 41, 46, 67–69, 74–81, 97,
103, 128, 131, 132, 136
cycle of, 22, 38, 138
domestic, 10, 22, 24–25, 29, 31–32,
34, 85
neighborhood, 23–25

Wacquant, Loic, 13–14, 54, 140–141
Weber, Max, 104, 107, 111, 141
ideal type, 4, 107

Welfare, 2, 3, 12–14, 99, 102, 133–134,
140
benefits, 99, 125
bureaucracy, 3,12
penal welfarism, 14
post-welfare society, 13, 53, 55
provisions, 3, 11–12, 16, 96
recipients, 14
reform, 8, 10, 12, 13, 20, 54–55,
104, 137
regime, 14, 96,
state, 1–3, 8, 10–12, 74, 102,
Western, Bruce, 10, 12, 20, 84, 136,
141
Wilson, William Julius, 2, 40, 50, 54,
141

Young Adult Offender (YAO), 4, 5,
10, 15,19, 23, 27, 68, 69, 100,
127